MW01029789

THE WEEKEND MPRE

Complete Preparation for the MPRE in Only a Weekend's Time

Third Edition

Leah Christensen
Professor of Legal Writing
University of San Diego School of Law

444 Cedar Street, Suite 700
St. Paul, MN 55101
1-877-888-1330

Printed in the United States of America

ISBN: 978-1-63659-294-7

This book is dedicated to Noah and Bailey Dean, my sons—who bring me more love and joy than I ever thought possible.

A Note on Sources

The MPRE tests knowledge, interpretation, and application of the ABA's Model Rules of Professional Conduct and the ABA's Model Code of Judicial Conduct. The ABA's Model Rules of Professional Conduct (and accompanying Comments) and the ABA's Model Code of Judicial Conduct (and accompanying Comments) have been adopted as official standards governing legal and judicial conduct in many states, including Delaware. Delaware has also adopted the numbering schemes used by the ABA for both sets of standards. The language and numbering schemes of both the Delaware Lawyers' Rules of Professional Conduct and the Delaware Judges' Code of Judicial Conduct are in the public domain. Thus, when using the exact expression of a Rule or Comment in this book (and in the related video series and supplementary material), the language used is from the Delaware Lawyers' Rules of Professional Conduct or the Delaware Judges' Code of Judicial Conduct.

TABLE OF CONTENTS

THE WEEKEND MPRE

Complete Preparation for the MPRE in Only a Weekend's Time

Third Edition

CHAPTER 1

AN INTRODUCTION TO THIS COURSE

Okay, the MPRE is coming up and you have no time at all. You're a busy 2L or 3L, and you need a fast, full-proof way to prepare for and pass the MPRE in the least amount of time required. Some of your classmates say you don't need to study at all. Other people say you need to study for a month before the MPRE to make sure you pass. But you have classes and a job, and you are already thinking about end-of-semester exams. And, of course, you've procrastinated! *And* you don't want to spend your time searching for and compiling good materials to prepare for the MPRE. Yes, there are free courses out there—lots of them. But is free always the best choice?

Perhaps you say, "I've taken Professional Responsibility, why do I need another class?" Often, Professional Responsibility (PR) courses provide you with the rules—but no real MPRE practice. Even if you've taken PR already in law school, you will probably not have all the materials you need from your PR class to prepare adequately for the MPRE. Ask anyone who has casually studied for the MPRE exam and failed (yes, people do fail the MPRE!). It is not an overly difficult exam, but it uses unique terminology and strange question formats. The multiple-choice questions on the MPRE are written differently than typical multiple-choice questions written by your professors or bar examiners. Think about MPRE questions being more like questions on the LSAT. There are a few important tricks to answering MPRE questions that can make your job as a test-taker far easier.

This mini-course is designed to provide you with the content you need to help you prepare for this very specific and focused practical exam. And this course is designed to give you LOTS of practice questions so you can begin to see the patterns that emerge from the questions that "trigger" specific rules. So, do you have a weekend? Of course you do! We can get you ready for your MPRE exam with a Friday to Sunday schedule—and you *will* pass using the methodology of this course.

What Is the MPRE?

Before diving into studying, you need to know about the exam you'll be taking. The MPRE is a sixty-question, 2 hour computer exam administered by the National Conference of Bar Examiners. The MPRE tests you on the disciplinary rules of professional conduct currently articulated in the ABA Model Rules of Professional Conduct and the ABA Model Code of Judicial Conduct. You will be bound by these rules when you become a licensed attorney. A passing score on the MPRE is required for admission to the bars in all but four U.S. jurisdictions. (You do not need a MPRE score for the jurisdictions of Wisconsin and Puerto Rico).

You have flexibility in determining when to take the MPRE (unlike the bar exam). Most students take the exam sometime after their second year of law school but before you begin studying for the bar. The exam is offered nationwide 3 times per year. If you prepare properly, you can take the MPRE even *before* you complete your law school course in Professional Responsibility. Unlike the bar exam, you can take the MPRE in any state and have your score submitted to another state. In fact, you don't even need to know where you will be taking the bar exam when you take the MPRE. You can transfer your score at a later date.

Overview of the MPRE Examination

The purpose of the MPRE is to measure your knowledge and understanding of the rules related to a lawyer's professional conduct; the MPRE does not test your *own* ethical values. Instead, the exam tests the standards the legal profession has deemed acceptable for how a lawyer is to act. As a lawyer, you may work in various roles: as a judge, an advocate or an advisor. These ethical rules apply to the work of lawyers in any of these roles.

Many law students think they will be able to recognize unethical behavior on the MPRE quite easily and, therefore, do not have to study for the MPRE. But the MPRE can be very tricky and the correct answer is not always clear. You need to know the rules well. You need to understand the intricacies of the rules. *And* you will also see that the Model Rules of Professional Responsibility are actually quite long and detailed (and you must read all the Comments to the rules as well). The rules and their application are not always intuitive.

The Weekend MPRE is designed to teach you the rules as they arise within the context of the MPRE and how to recognize the specific fact patterns that trigger a specific rule. It was also created to provide, in one place, everything you need to pass the MPRE, including lots of practice questions.

How Does *The Weekend MPRE* Use Learning Theory to Your Benefit?

The MPRE exam is not a law school exam. Studying for the MPRE will be easier than studying for the bar exam or a law school essay exam, but you do need to attack the exam efficiently. Too many students fail the MPRE one, two, or even three times—because they don't study the right materials. Then test anxiety sets in and it becomes even harder to pass the exam.

The Weekend MPRE has designed a comprehensive program of outlines, lectures, and testing materials to maximize your ability to pass the MPRE the first time. The key is to study efficiently and to *practice* the MPRE-style questions in addition to learning the rules.

Educational studies have demonstrated that the best system for retention of material involves learning a topic, moving on to other information, and then coming back to that initial topic and re-learning through repetition. When you follow this method, used by *The Weekend MPRE,* you activate the learning process. Your first step will be to review the substantive law, the Rules of Professional Conduct, by reviewing the rules themselves. You will review the comments to the rules which provide examples that are often tested in the MPRE. You will then listen to short lectures (and follow along with condensed mini-outlines). The lectures will discuss how to specifically decode an MPRE question. Following the substantive lectures, you will take short quizzes using MPRE-like, multiple-choice test questions to enhance your understanding of the rules. This approach will reinforce your knowledge by providing multiple opportunities for review. Finally, you will practice with full-length MPRE simulated exams—so you can practice timing and pacing as well as substantive knowledge.

The methodology used here is efficient, active, and engaging. Educational research shows that adult learners need this type of learning framework to retain information for exams.

What's the Format of This Course?

This mini-course is based upon completing the following tasks: (1) thoroughly reading the rules and Comments to the rules; (2) actively listening to short lectures; (3) practicing with short quizzes; and (4) practicing with full-length, simulated MPRE exams. It is more helpful to start with quizzes rather than full-length exams. Studies have shown that learning is enhanced by doing groups of 5 questions, then reviewing the answers in detail versus practicing only with full length exams.

1. Reading the Rules

Yes, you must read the rules thoroughly from front to back, including the Comments following the rules. You must also read the Judicial Code of Conduct. This "reading" step will actually be the most time-consuming aspect of preparing for the exam. The ABA Model Rules of Professional Responsibility are very long and complex. Your job is to read them through, and then to outline the most important elements of each rule so that you understand the rules at their most basic level. Some are more straightforward than others. But all may be tested. Once you read the rules through once or twice, you won't have to look at them again during your preparation.

2. Active Listening to the Lectures

You will then listen to 15 short lectures that correspond to the short outlines in the book. The lectures are typically designed to last no longer than 10 minutes each. Learning theory tells us that, in a lecture format, students can retain only about 20 minutes' worth of complex material at any time. So, we have designed these lectures specifically to maximize your retention and understanding of the material.

Your listening and participation must be active. Listen to the lectures *with the outlines in front of you.* Mark up the outlines with the strategies and insights you hear in the lectures.

3. Short Quiz Sessions to Build Knowledge

After each lecture, you will answer a series of online multiple-choice questions, written to simulate actual MPRE questions that are designed to test your knowledge of the subject matter you just reviewed. There are approximately 5 questions per lesson, followed by detailed explanations. The quiz questions will test your grasp of the information, and the explanations will further enhance your knowledge. With only 5 questions per lesson or lesson group, you can take your time to really review the questions and their answers to achieve maximum retention of the subject matter.

4. Simulated MPRE Exams

The final component of this course is to simulate (in both time and content) the actual MPRE testing experience. Research has shown that students who *practice* taking an exam in a simulated test environment improve their scores *substantially* on the actual exam. This course contains two full, MPRE-like exams so you can get a sense of the timing required for the MPRE, the complexity of questions, and the pacing of the exam. You will also be able to determine the subject areas in which you struggle, thereby allowing you to do some additional practice on weaker areas before the exam.

Recently, I had a student come see me shortly after failing the MPRE. I was surprised that this student had not passed the MPRE on the first time—he was an excellent student in law school. The student was very frustrated and described how he reviewed the rules over and over again before taking the MPRE. I asked him whether he had *practiced* taking any MPRE exams before the exam itself. He looked up surprised and responded that he had *not* practiced the actual MPRE questions—he had focused solely on the rules. That was the problem! This student needed to practice the MPRE questions just as much as he focused on the individual rules. Practicing the questions allows you to see and recognize the patterns that appear frequently on the MPRE exam.

What Is the Weekend Schedule?

How should you plan your weekend the Saturday *before* the MPRE? Here's our suggestion for a plan that you can tailor to meet your individual needs. We go into our plan in much more detail at the end of this Introduction—this is just the basics!

Friday: 5 p.m. to 8 p.m.

Read the ABA Model Rules of Professional Responsibility and the Judicial Code of Conduct.

Saturday: 9 a.m. to 12 noon.

Lessons 1–8:

Review outlines and listen to lectures; take and review quizzes.

Saturday afternoon: 2 p.m. to 5 p.m.

Lessons 9–16:

Review outlines and listen to lectures; take and review quizzes.

Sunday: 9 a.m. to 11 a.m.

Lessons 17–20:

Review outlines and listen to lectures; take and review quizzes.

Sunday: 1 p.m. to 5 p.m.

MPRE Simulated Exam 1:

Review of Incorrect Answers.

MPRE Simulated Exam 2:

Review of Incorrect Answers.

Why Is *The Weekend MPRE* Different from Other, *Free* Prep Courses?

You will see advertisements for free MPRE courses from commercial bar prep providers. The commercial bar companies offer MPRE courses as a supplement to their bar programs. The information in these courses is good, but it may not be *all* the information you need to pass the MPRE on the first take. Usually, these programs offer one lecture that is about two hours long and some study questions.

Ask any upper-level law student and you will discover that the MPRE can be tricky. It is not difficult, but it is unique. There are some law students—even those in the tops of their classes—who struggle with the MPRE precisely because it is NOT like any other exam in law school. It may be a multiple-choice exam, but the questions are very different from those on a typical law school, multiple-choice exam. Think about how strange the questions on the LSAT were at first. The phrases used on the MPRE can be unusual. The calls of the questions are both specific and unique. You can discover this yourself by taking the exam more than once or you can master the MPRE in a weekend by using this course.

You do need more substantive preparation than simply reviewing the Professional Responsibility rules several times over the weekend prior to the MPRE exam. But you do not need to study for the MPRE weeks on end like you will for the bar exam.

This course is meant to be efficient, entertaining, and effective. You will receive condensed outlines. The lectures will be short to maximize your retention. Further, instead of just presenting the substantive law, the lectures will focus on skills—how do you properly decode an MPRE question? What does the term "knowledge" mean in the MPRE exam? In short, this course gathers everything you need to know about the MPRE into one place so you can pass the first time.

CHAPTER 2

BASIC INFORMATION ABOUT THE MPRE

The MPRE is created and administered by the NCBE, which is also responsible for the Multistate Bar Examination. The MPRE is currently administered in every state, as well as the District of Columbia. All but two jurisdictions require the MPRE to obtain a law license in the state. Wisconsin and Puerto Rico do not require the MPRE in order to be a member of the bar.

The MPRE is offered three times a year: in March, August, and November. In many states, you can take the MPRE before you finish law school; ideally, you should take the MPRE as soon as you complete your course in Professional Responsibility, and take it early enough so that if you do fail, you'll have another chance to take it before the bar exam (some states will not let you sit for the bar exam until after you have passed the MPRE). Some of your classmates will tell you that you "don't need your PR course" to take the MPRE. That is true, IF you are diligent and take the time necessary to study the Model Rules of Professional Conduct. The MPRE is different than typical law school exams. Although the rules are important in law school exams, the focus is actually on the application and analysis of the facts applied to those rules in law school. For the MPRE, the rules are the focus of the exam. You are not asked to do written analysis in the MPRE. Instead, you examine a fact pattern and determine which rule applies as well as assessing how it applies.

All of the questions on the MPRE—60 in total—are multiple-choice questions. You will take the exam on a computer. Not all questions are scored; 10 out of the 60 questions are "pretest" questions that are not scored. The pretest questions are not identified, so test-takers cannot tell which questions on their exam will or will not be scored Therefore, it is critical to answer all 60 questions.

You will have two hours in which to answer these questions.

What Do the Questions Cover?

The questions on the MPRE cover both judicial and attorney conduct. This is important to understand since most professional responsibility courses do not cover the Judicial Code of Conduct. The MPRE questions covering judicial ethics require you to know the current ABA Model Code of Judicial Conduct (CJC). The Judicial Code of Conduct is very similar to the ABA Model Rules of Professional Responsibility (the "Model Rules") but you do need to read the Judicial Code specifically.

Most of the questions on the MPRE, however, cover attorney conduct. You will need to know the current Model Rules for the questions about lawyer discipline. The exam also includes questions that go beyond lawyer discipline. Such questions, in the words of the NCBE, "are designed to measure an understanding of the generally accepted rules, principles, and common law regulating the legal profession in the United States." For these questions, you will look to the established norms within the professional conduct of lawyers.

The MPRE does not test your knowledge of a specific jurisdictions' statutes or rules. But some questions may require you to apply a local statute or rule that has been incorporated into the text of the question.

How Is the MPRE Scored?

Your MPRE score is determined by how many questions you answer correctly; there's no penalty for incorrect answers. The lesson to be learned is this: it pays to answer *every* question, even if you're not exactly sure what the correct answer is. In addition, your overall score is scaled against the scores of other test takers—so you cannot actually guess the correct number of questions you need to answer in order to achieve a particular score.

How Do I Apply for the MPRE?

To apply for the MPRE, go the website of the National Conference of Bar Examiners—you can apply easily online. One tip: think about WHERE you want to take the exam. Even though the exam is now taken on a computer, you still need to go to a specific site.

What Is the Scope of the Exam?

Questions about the professional responsibility rules related to lawyer conduct make up approximately 54–56 questions on the MPRE. The remaining questions test your knowledge of judicial conduct.

The NCBE site lists the items tested in an outline format. Occasionally an exam may include other items, but the NCBE's outline gives you a good clue as to what will be tested on the exam. Not all of the items listed below are tested every time, but if you've covered them all in your studies, you can't miss!

The approximate number of questions per subject are as follows:

1. Regulation of the legal profession (5 questions)
2. The client-lawyer relationship (7 questions)
3. Client confidentiality (8 questions)
4. Conflicts of interest (10 questions), arbitrator, mediator, or other third-party neutral
5. Competence, legal malpractice, and other civil liability (6 questions)
6. Litigation and other forms of advocacy (8 questions)
7. Transactions and communications with persons other than clients (3 questions)
8. Different roles of the lawyer (4 questions)
9. Safekeeping funds and other property (4 questions)
10. Communications about legal services (5 questions)

What Are the Questions Like?

Each MPRE question consists of a fact scenario or hypothetical followed by a question (also known as a "call" or a "prompt"). You then have to select the "best" answer choice from among four choices. Remember: your score is determined by the number of questions you answer correctly. You will not be penalized for wrong answers so answer every question!

Here's an example of a typical MPRE question:

An attorney represented a buyer in a corporate transaction. Due to the attorney's negligence in drafting the corporate bylaws, the client was required to pay penalties from the state. The attorney fully disclosed this negligence to the client and the client suggested that he would be satisfied if the attorney simply reimbursed the client for the cost of the penalties. Although the client might have recovered additional damages if a malpractice action were filed, the attorney reasonably believed that the proposed settlement was fair to the buyer. Accordingly, in order to prevent a malpractice action, the attorney readily agreed to make the reimbursement. The attorney drafted a settlement agreement, and it was executed by both the attorney and the client.

Was the attorney's conduct proper?

(A) Yes, if the attorney advised the client in writing that the client should seek independent representation before deciding to agree to the settlement offer.

(B) Yes, because the attorney reasonably believed that the proposed settlement was fair to the buyer.

(C) No, because the attorney settled a case involving liability for malpractice while the matter was still ongoing.

(D) No, unless the buyer was separately represented in negotiating and finalizing the settlement agreement.

Here, the correct answer is A.

Note that in this question, the first paragraph is the fact pattern or "root" of the question. Note further that in recent MPRE exams, the fact patterns have become longer and longer. Therefore, you need to practice working through the fact patterns to develop your ability to read and assess the facts efficiently. Time is not usually a problem in the MPRE exam. In other words, you do not need to rush through these questions as you may have done on a law school exam. You have the time to read the facts carefully.

The final sentence, "Was the attorney's conduct proper?" is called the "call" of the question. The "call" tells you specifically what to look for in the answer options. The answer choices, A through D, are called "answer options." One of the answers is the "best" response (note, it may not be the *only* correct answer). The other three answer choices are called "distractors." "Distractors" are answer choices that are written so like a correct answer that they will "distract" you from the best answer. One key tip is to always read the "call" of the question first before you jump into the fact pattern. You want to know the focus of the question before you read through the fact pattern.

How Should You Attack the Fact Patterns?

The fact patterns can be long and very detailed, so you need a plan for how you will attack them. You will have about two minutes to read each question, answer it, and move on. This means that you must have a strong grasp of all the rules; there's no time to waste trying to remember which rule is which. Further, you must be able to read through the fact patterns efficiently.

To help you do this, you need to teach yourself what to look for. This process is called finding the "trigger facts" in any question—those legally significant facts that "trigger" the legal issues within each question. You learn "trigger facts" by doing lots of practice questions. You will begin to see patterns of facts that consistently trigger specific rules.

Remember that the MPRE is actually very limited in the range and types of issues it tests. Given that the exam is multiple-choice, the MPRE cannot always test gray areas within the professional responsibility rules well—the facts and rules usually point to one best answer. Students familiar with the MPRE often suggest that if you are stuck on a question, pick the second most ethical answer. In other words, one of the key distractor questions will be what on its fact appears to be the most ethical answer. Often, this is not the best answer—because lawyers realistically have competing considerations involved in any ethics decision. The "perfect" answer ethically is not always the best answer.

Further, there are a limited number of fact patterns that the examiners can come up with, because they are testing not only you, but also every other law student in the country, regardless of state or background. Therefore, the test sticks to the main issues and rarely tests obscure issues. Consequently, the more you practice, the more you will be able to recognize patterns and "trigger facts" amongst the questions. In this sense, the MPRE is easier than a typical law school exam. However, it takes efficient and focused studying to ensure you pass the first time.

What Are Some Unique Phrases and/or Definitions Specifically Used in the MPRE?

Okay, this part is important! You need to understand the specific phrases used in the MPRE to effectively master the MPRE exam. This is often something that students bypass when studying for the MPRE, yet it is crucial.

Questions will often include the following words or phrases, which have very specific meanings within the context of the MPRE:

- "*Subject to discipline*" asks whether the conduct described in the question would subject the lawyer to discipline under the provisions of the ABA Model Rules of Professional Conduct. In the case of a judge, the test question asks whether the judge would be subject to discipline under the ABA Model Code of Judicial Conduct.
- "*May*" or "*proper*" asks whether the conduct referred to or described in the question is professionally appropriate in that it would not result in a rule violation.
- "*Subject to litigation sanction*" asks whether the conduct would subject the lawyer or the lawyer's law firm to a sanction by a tribunal such as a fine, fee forfeiture, disqualification, punishment for contempt, or other sanction.

- "*Subject to civil liability*" asks whether the conduct would subject the lawyer or the lawyer's law firm to civil liability, such as malpractice, misrepresentation, or breach of fiduciary duty.
- "*Subject to criminal liability*" asks whether the conduct would subject the lawyer to criminal liability for participation in criminal acts, such as prosecution for insurance or tax fraud, destruction of evidence, or obstruction of justice.

What Are Other Important Phrases on the MPRE?

In order to prepare for the MPRE, you want to learn not only the professional responsibility rules, but also how to recognize important phraseology within the MPRE questions themselves. There are particular statements or themes brought forth in MPRE questions that you will see over and over again. Consider the following:

1. <u>What Is the Lawyer's or Client's State of Mind?</u>

In many of the professional responsibility rules, a lawyer only violates the rule if a lawyer *knows* the conduct is wrong. Note words in a question such as "knows," or "knowingly," or "becomes convinced," or "believes," or "reasonably believes."

Pay attention to the MPRE's description of the attorney's state of mind, i.e., his or her beliefs and knowledge, in determining whether or not he or she has acted ethically.

2. <u>Why Did the Lawyer Act or Fail to Act?</u>

Just like you want to pay attention to the lawyer's state of mind, you also want to examine the lawyer's motivation for acting or not acting in any given situation.

Consider the following example. Let's assume there's a question dealing with permissive or mandatory withdrawal from representation. Is the attorney withdrawing because of moral reasons? Financial reasons? The attorney's reasons for withdrawing will be crucial in determining whether or not the withdrawal is ultimately ethical under the rules.

Or what about the situation in which a lawyer needs to decide whether or not to call a particular witness at trial?

Typically, whether or not to call a witness is within the scope of authority of the attorney, not the client, under Rule 1.2. Under normal circumstances, the attorney has acted properly if he or she decides not to call a witness after careful thought. But if the facts suggest that the lawyer decided not to call a witness because it would take too much time or require too much preparation, these motivations would raise a question about whether the attorney violated the duty of competence and the duty of diligence under Rules 1.1 and 1.3.

When a question asks about the attorney's motivations, then you have to analyze those motivations carefully to determine whether the behavior itself was proper.

3. Pay Attention to the Lawyer's Actions

In some MPRE questions, the examiners test your knowledge of the ethical rules by dressing up "bad" behavior with "good" behavior. The examiners use this strategy to determine if you know that adding "good" behavior does not take away from the original unethical conduct. Consider an attorney's duty of competence under Rule 1.1. A question that asks, "Is a lawyer subject to discipline for providing incompetent service," without other facts, would not lead anyone to answer "no" to that question.

But suppose the lawyer tells the client that he is not competent to handle a matter, and the client insists that he handle it anyway, because the client trusts only that one lawyer over all others. Even in this situation—where the lawyer is doing exactly what the client wants—the lawyer will be found to have violated the ethical rules by taking on a case for which the lawyer is not competent. Simply adding facts, i.e., the client's insistence on to the lawyer's handling of the work, does not change an unethical action into an appropriate one.

One of the examiner's most common ways to trick you is by trying to distract you from the right answer by "fixing" the rule violation with a good outcome or client consent. Be wary of questions that use this type of fact pattern and answer options.

4. Don't Be Tricked by a Question That "Solves" the Unethical Conduct by "Dressing" It up with Good Conduct

This is a very common MPRE trap—the facts describe conduct by a lawyer that is wrong, but then tell you that the misconduct has not affected the client. When this happens in an MPRE question, you can bet that at least one of the distractor facts will suggest that the lawyer's conduct was proper because his client wasn't "prejudiced" or "adversely affected." Even if things work out fine for the client, the lawyer may still be subject to discipline for violating the rules in the first place. Once a lawyer has engaged in unethical conduct, it doesn't really matter what the consequence of that conduct is to the client; the lawyer has violated the rules and he or she is subject to discipline. (Note: this is different from a malpractice action, where in order to recover, the client *does* have to experience damage).

5. Less Is Always More When You're Dealing with Attorney's Fees

The MPRE often asks questions about attorney's fees that are in dispute between a lawyer and a client. The Rule (Rule 1.5(a)) states broadly that a lawyer's fee shall be "reasonable." Therefore, in a question asking about attorney's fees, it's likely that the lower fee will be perceived as more reasonable. Thus, when a question asks what part of a fee a lawyer may properly keep, you're probably safe if you opt for the choice that best protects the client's interests in the money under dispute.

6. Even if a Client "Wants" a Course of Action, the Lawyer Must Still Follow the Rules

Sometimes an MPRE fact pattern will feature an attorney who has violated the rules at the request of the client. Remember: the client's insistence on improper conduct by the lawyer does not relieve the lawyer of the obligation *not* to engage in the conduct.

Eliminate Wrong Answers

One of the most important skills you can bring with you to the MPRE is the ability to identify when an answer is clearly wrong. Once you know how to eliminate the wrong answers, you'll be able to pick out the right answer every time. Consider the following tips for eliminating wrong answers:

1. If you see the right answer, choose it!

2. If an answer is strangely written or if you know it's clearly wrong, then quickly eliminate it.

3. Watch out for answer options that misstate a rule or facts from the question—or have facts in the answer choice that contradict facts from the hypothetical.

4. If you run across an answer choice that sounds too familiar, this could be a well-written distractor. Make sure every aspect of the answer is correct.

5. If the ethical issue jumps out at you, don't get distracted by what appears to be an easy issue. Occasionally, there are easy questions. Read the "call" of the question carefully to make sure you're addressing the actual issue being tested.

General Test-Taking Strategies to Enhance Your Success

The lectures and outlines will provide valuable test-taking tips specifically focused on the MPRE. But here are a few general thoughts and strategies about the exam.

1. Avoid Taking the Test at a Test Site Near Your Law School

There could be lots of stressed-out students trying to do the same thing on the same day. Schedule the test at a location just a bit farther away from your school.

2. Don't Over-Prepare

Taking *The Weekend MPRE* is the perfect amount of preparation. In reality, you can prepare effectively in one weekend. It's really the number of total number of hours you put into your studying rather than the number of days or weeks.

3. Take the MPRE a Year Before You Take the Bar

Most students, if they had to do it again, would tell you to take the exam the year before you take the bar exam—typically the summer between your second and third year is ideal.

Okay, let's begin!

CHAPTER 3

THE SCHEDULE

You can adapt the schedule below to fit your needs. Perhaps you want to do two hours a day for five days? That's fine. Our proposed schedule offers you segmented study sessions that you can complete in a weekend—or however you would like.

What Is the Weekend Schedule?

How should you plan your weekend before the MPRE? Here's our suggestion for a plan that you can tailor to meet your individual needs.

Friday: 5 p.m. to 8 p.m.

Read over the ABA Model Rules of Professional Responsibility (including definitions) and the Judicial Code of Conduct. Take notes, and actively mark up the Rule Book!

This is an essential part of your preparation because it gives you the basis for the short lectures. If you have time, read through the rules thoroughly once, then skim through them a second time.

Saturday: 9 a.m. to 12 noon

Saturday will be spent primarily listening to the 10-minute lectures as you read through the outlines. You will need to actively listen and write in your outlines as you hear the additional information within the lectures to gain important content. Remember that the outlines only serve as a guide. The primary content for this course is given in the lectures.

Lessons 1 and 2: **Test Strategies for the MPRE and Areas of Coverage**

Review Outlines (10 minutes)

Listen to Lectures (10 minutes each × 2 = 20 minutes)

Take Quiz and Review Answers (20 minutes)

5 Minute Break! Get up and Stretch!

Total: 55 minutes

Lesson 3: **The Framework for the MPRE**

Review Outline (5 minutes)

Listen to Lecture (10 minutes)

No Quiz Questions

Total: 15 Minutes

Lessons 4 and 5: **The Judicial Code of Conduct and Outside Activities of Judges**

Review Outlines (10 minutes)

Listen to Lectures (20 minutes)

Take Quiz and Review Answers (10 minutes)

5 Minute Break! Get up and Stretch!

Total: 45 minutes

Lessons 6 and 7: **Lying and Acting Badly and Practicing Without a License**

Review Outline (10 minutes)

Listen to Lecture (20 minutes)

Take Quiz and Review Answers (10 minutes)

5 Minute Break! Get up and Stretch!

Total: 45 minutes

BREAK: Noon to 2 p.m.

Saturday Afternoon: 2 p.m. to 5 p.m.

Lesson 8: **Competence and Diligence**

Review Outline (5 minutes)

Listen to Lecture (10 minutes)

Take Quiz and Review Answers (10 minutes)

Total: 25 Minutes

Lesson 9: **Trust Accounts**

Review Outline (5 minutes)

Listen to Lecture (10 minutes)

Take Quiz and Review Answers (5 minutes)

5 Minute Break! Get up and Stretch!

Total: 25 minutes

Lessons 10 and 11: **Advertising and Solicitation**

Review Outlines (10 minutes)

Listen to Lecture (10 minutes)

Take Quiz and Review Answers (10 minutes)

Total: 30 minutes

Lessons 12 and 13: **Attorney's Fees and Limitation on Right to Practice**

Review Outlines (10 minutes)

Listen to Lecture (10 minutes)

Take Quiz and Review Answers (10 minutes)

Total: 30 minutes

Lesson 14: **Conflicts of Interest: Concurrent**

Review Outline (5 minutes)

Listen to Lecture (10 minutes)

Take Quiz and Review Answers (10 minutes)

Total: 25 minutes

Lesson 15: **Conflicts of Interest: Corporations**

Review Outline (5 minutes)

Listen to Lecture (10 minutes)

No Quiz

Total: 15 minutes

Lesson 16: **Conflicts of Interest: Former Clients and Imputation**

Review Outline (10 minutes)

Listen to Lecture (10 minutes)

Take Quiz and Review Answers (10 minutes)

5 Minute Break! Get up and Stretch!

Total: 35 minutes

Sunday: 9 a.m. to 11 a.m.

Lesson 17: **The Duty of Confidentiality and the Attorney-Client Relationship**

Review Outline (10 minutes)

Listen to Lecture (10 minutes)

Take Quiz and Review Answers (10 minutes)

Total: 30 minutes

Lesson 18: **Zealous Representation**

Review Outline (5 minutes)

Listen to Lecture (10 minutes)

Take Quiz and Review Answers (10 minutes)

Total: 25 minutes

Lessons 19 and 20: **Candor Toward the Tribunal and Termination of the Attorney-Client Relationship**

Review Outlines (10 minutes)

Listen to Lecture (10 minutes)

Take Quiz and Review Answers (10 minutes)

Total: 30 minutes

BREAK: 11 a.m. to 1 p.m.

Sunday: 1 p.m. to 5 p.m.

MPRE Simulated Exam 1: 60 minutes

Review of Incorrect Answers: 60 minutes

Total: 120 minutes

MPRE Simulated Exam 2: 60 minutes

Review of Incorrect Answers: 60 minutes

Total: 120 minutes

Note that we offer our quizzes in an online format (within the website). The simulated MPRE exams are offered in both the online format and written format (at the end of this booklet). The actual MPRE is in a fully online format.

Are you ready to get started? We'll get you prepared for the MPRE in just a weekend! Let's do it!

CHAPTER 4

THE WEEKEND MPRE OUTLINES

Lessons 1–20

Lesson 1
Test Strategies for the MPRE

I. <u>THE MPRE: A UNIQUE EXAM</u>

A. <u>An Attitude of Confidence Produces Success</u>

B. <u>Technique Is More Important than Knowledge of Specific Rules</u>

C. <u>Complete the Test—Sixty Questions in Two Hours</u>

1. No award for speed.
2. Technique, alone, should account for many correct answers—and that should get you over the top.
3. Your score is determined by how many questions you answer correctly; no penalty for incorrect answers. Answer every question!!

D. <u>A Reason Why You Should Answer Every Question</u>

1. No penalty for a wrong answer.

E. <u>Step-by-Step Approach</u>

1. Read the call twice—be careful of the "negative" call.
2. Read the facts.
3. Attempt to determine the answer *before* reading the options (but if cannot, okay).
   a. Remember the three most-common types of incorrect options:
      1) Incorrect statement of law or fact.

2) Overbroad options: too general.

3) Incorrect reasoning in answer option.

b. Proper = good; May = acceptable.

4. Eliminate wrong answers immediately; eliminate incorrect letters.

5. Choose the best of the remaining "mediocre" answers.

a. Note: If you cannot decide, the more specific answer is usually better.

b. Correct answer may be the "least worst," "none of the above" or a minority position. (If you have no idea, find the most ethical answer and choose the second one that seems slightly less perfect).

6. Timing: two minutes to read each question, answer it, and move on. Keep moving.

F. Special Approach for "Multiple True/False" Questions: (The dreaded roman numerals).

1. Analyze each Roman numeral as if it were a "true/false" question (Remember: a big problem is just a set of little problems.)

2. Eliminate options that contain one or more false Roman numerals.

G. People Do Fail the MPRE: Start by knowing the rules, then practice.

H. What Does the MPRE Test Cover? Questions on the ABA Model Rules make up approximately 55 out of the 60 questions on the MPRE. The NCBE's outline of MPRE subjects states the approximately weight given to each topic:

1. Regulation of the Legal Profession (5 questions)

(Admission to the Profession, Lawyer Discipline, Reporting of Professional Misconduct; Unauthorized Practice of Law; Multi-Jurisdictional Practice; Fee Division; Law Firm Practice; Responsibilities of Partners, Supervisory, etc.; Restrictions on the Right to Practice).

2. The Lawyer-Client Relationship (7 questions)

   (Formation of Lawyer-Client Relationship; Scope of Representation; Decision-Making Authority; Counseling; Termination of the Lawyer-Client Relationship; Communications with Clients; Fees).

3. Client Confidentiality (8 questions)

   (Attorney-Client Privilege; Work Product; Confidentiality; Disclosures Authorized by Client; Exceptions to Confidentiality).

4. Conflicts of Interest (10 questions)

   (Current Client Conflicts; Personal Interest Conflicts; Former Client; Prospective Clients; Imputed Conflicts; Business Transactions with Clients; Third-Party Compensation).

5. Competence, Legal Malpractice, and Other Civil Liability (6 questions)

   (Competence; Expediting Litigation; Candor to the Tribunal; Fairness to Opposition; Trial Publicity; Lawyer as a Witness).

6. Litigation and Other Forms of Advocacy (8 questions)

   (Meritorious Claims; Expediting Litigation; Candor to the Tribunal; Fairness to Parties).

7. Transactions and Communications with Persons Other than Clients (3 questions)

8. Different Roles of the Lawyer (3 questions)

   (Advisor, Evaluator, Negotiator, Arbitrator, Prosecutors).

9. Safekeeping Funds and Other Property (4 questions)

   (Client Trust Accounts; Safekeeping Funds; Property of Clients).

10. Communication About Legal Services (4 questions)

    (Advertising; Solicitation; Group Legal Services; Referrals; Fields of Practice).

11. Lawyers' Duties to the Legal System (1 question)

    (Voluntary Prop Bono; Accepting Appointments; Serving in LSO's).

12. Judicial Ethics (2 questions)

    (Independence of the Judiciary; Duties of Judicial Office; Ex Parte Communications; Disqualification).

Lesson 2
The Examiner's Purpose and Areas of Coverage

A. Test Examinee's Ability to Spot Ethical Problems and Avoid/Solve

   1. Note Common Mistake: Thinking morals or real life. Instead, Think "Code" (loyalty to Court, client, then society).

B. State Law: Not tested on MPRE. Presently, MPRE passing scores in the most states range from 70 to 85. California presently requires a scaled score of 86.

C. The MPRE Tests: Primarily the Model Rules of Professional Conduct; the Model Code of Judicial Conduct; leading constitutional legal ethics cases; and common law/majority cross-over issues concerning civil procedure [e.g., sanctions], torts [e.g., legal malpractice], criminal law [e.g., embezzlement of client funds], and evidence [e.g., attorney-client privilege].

   Mandatory vs. Discretionary Conduct

   1. "Mandatory" Conduct:

      a. If willful violation, or pattern of violations, attorney is subject to discipline.

      b. Key Words: "must," "shall," "subject to discipline," "disciplinary rule," "subject to litigation sanction," "subject to disqualification," "subject to civil liability," and "subject to criminal liability."

   2. "Discretionary" Conduct:

      a. Aspirational; no discipline.

      b. Key Words: "should," "may," "proper," and "appropriate."

   3. Approach: Our focus is the mandatory conduct. So if it seems unfamiliar, the correct answer is probably "may,"

"proper," "should," "not subject to discipline," or "appropriate."

4. Elimination of Wrong Answers:

   a. Pay special attention to statements about the lawyer's or the client's state of mind.

      In many ethics rules, the propriety of a lawyer's conduct depends on whether he or she knows or believes something. Pay attention to words or phrases like "knows," "knowingly," "concludes," "becomes convinced," "believes," and "reasonably believes."

      Ask: did the lawyer know the true facts at the time he or she made the recommendation? If not, then he or she is not subject to discipline!

Lesson 3
The Framework of the Model Rules of Professional Responsibility

Is Professional Responsibility a billion arbitrary rules? Yes and no . . .

I. THE ETHICAL TENSIONS TESTED BY THE MPRE

A. Tension #1: Client vs. Court [choose Court, e.g., perjury; contrary law]

B. Tension #2: Client vs. Client [if actual conflict, attorney and firm are out]

C. Tension #3: Client vs. Society [choose Client except if future dangerous crime or future fraud]

D. The Hierarchy of Lawyer Loyalties

1. Court
2. Client
3. Society

E. Approach

1. Learn the underlying rationale for a subject; this will allow you to figure out the correct rules.
2. If a question seems strange, it is just one of the above rules in disguise—or it is "proper" conduct.
3. Pay attention to the lawyer's core behavior. The examiners may try to test your knowledge of ethical rules by surrounding unethical behavior with the "trappings" of propriety. Strip embellishments away and ask what's really going on. Start with undisputed facts and work your way up from there.

4. Other considerations regarding typically wrong answers:
   a. When it comes to fees, less is typically better.
   b. If a rule forbids communication between two persons, it doesn't matter who initiates the communication.
   c. An attorney may not engage in conduct that would cause a judge to violate the Code of Judicial Conduct.
   d. A client's insistence on a course of conduct doesn't relieve the lawyer of the responsibility to observe the rules.

II. DISCIPLINE VS. MALPRACTICE

Read the call of question carefully to determine whether the issue is discipline or malpractice:

A. Discipline

1. Discipline is neither civil nor criminal.
2. It is an administrative action undertaken by the state bar to protect the public from dangerously bad lawyers. Thus, only licensed attorneys are subject to discipline.
3. The purpose: Protect the public from dangerously corrupt or inept attorneys.
4. The *mens rea* for discipline is "willful," i.e., recklessness or a pattern of neglect. No discipline for first-time good faith error.
5. Four types of discipline: (First-time good faith mistakes probably will not subject the attorney to discipline. Rather, a pattern of violation is necessary.)
   a. Private reprimand
   b. Public reprimand
   c. Suspension
   d. Disbarment
6. Attorney has a right to notice and hearing, but may have to prove own good character.

7. Jurisdiction (Rule 8.5): A lawyer is subject to the disciplinary authority of the jurisdiction in which he or she is licensed even when engaged in conduct elsewhere.

B. Malpractice

1. Malpractice is a tort—it is a specific type of negligence. Discipline is not malpractice.

2. Negligence is the most common theory:

   a. Breach of the standard of care owed, and that breach caused damages.

   b. Standard of Care: Malpractice requires merely objective error—good faith no defense.

      1) Where defendant is a professional (possesses knowledge or skill greater than average person), the "reasonable person" to whom compared is a member of the trade with the "customary" level of special knowledge of one in good standing; not "average" skill.

      2) "Specialists" are held to higher standard.

   c. Breach of Duty of Due Care: An attorney is not liable for mere errors of judgment. The failure to find the answer to a legal question is a breach if reasonably competent legal research would have revealed the answer.

   d. Damages: Direct losses and indirect but foreseeable losses. (Note: if the plaintiff's case was a "loser," there will be no damages.) You must have damages in order for an attorney to be found to have committed malpractice!

   e. Liability for Negligence of Others: Lawyer can be liable for damages caused by negligent secretaries, clerks, etc. (Discipline would require a failure to train/supervise.)

Lesson 4
Judicial Conduct

I. THE MODEL RULES DO NOT AFFECT THE MODEL CODE OF JUDICIAL CONDUCT; THEY ARE SEPARATE

II. JUDGES ARE HELD TO A HIGHER STANDARD

A. Uphold integrity and independence of judiciary. (Canon 1; Rule 1.2).

B. Avoid appearance of impropriety in all activities as determined by an objective test. (Canon 2).

   1. Code of Judicial Conduct 2.3: Avoid bias, prejudice, and harassment; duty to prevent lawyers from engaging in this behavior.

C. Do not discriminate in any way—on or off bench. (Canon 2).

D. Note the scope: some questions will frame issue in terms of "may" or "should." The conduct in question is left to the personal and professional discretion of the judge.

III. JUDGES MUST AVOID THE APPEARANCE OF IMPROPRIETY

A. No voluntary appearance as a character witness. (Code of Judicial Conduct 3.3).

B. No discriminatory organizations. (Code of Judicial Conduct 3.6).

C. No use of nonpublic information. (Code of Judicial Conduct 3.5).

D. No practice of law. (Code of Judicial Conduct 3.10).

E. No compensation for extrajudicial activities. (Code of Judicial Conduct 3.11).

F. No ex parte communication. (Code of Judicial Ethics 2.9).

Note that a judge cannot receive *ex parte* communications, except on non-substantive matters, like scheduling. If judge receives anything, must promptly notify parties.

G. No extrajudicial statements. A judge shall not make any extrajudicial statement about the status of a pending matter. (Code of Judicial Conduct 2.10).

IV. JUDGES MAY RECEIVE LIMITED COMPENSATION AS LONG AS IT DOESN'T APPEAR IMPROPER

A. Report compensation from other activities. (Code of Judicial Conduct 3.15).

B. Judges cannot be compensated when working for non-family or non-personal corporations—however, law teaching/lecturing/writing is okay. (Code of Judicial Conduct 3.12).

C. Reimbursement for expenses must be limited to the actual cost of travel, lodging, etc. (Code of Judicial Conduct 3.14).

D. Judges can receive compensation for extrajudicial activities but the standard is reasonableness! (Code of Judicial Conduct Rule 3.12).

Lesson 5
Judicial Conduct: Outside Activities

I. NON-JUDICIAL ACTIVITIES

A. Avocational: Most okay if no impropriety or does not detract from dignity of office. (Code of Judicial Conduct 3.7).

B. Civic/Charitable: Okay if they do not interfere or reflect adversely. (Code of Judicial Conduct 3.7):

1. Can serve as officer, etc. of group if not conducted for its own economic/political advantage.
2. Can indirectly assist in raising/managing funds but cannot personally participate in public fundraising.
3. Do not give legal or financial advice.

C. Financial Activities: Judges must be "above-board" and fair. Watch out for fact patterns involving impropriety/conflicts (e.g. gifts/loans). (Code of Judicial Conduct 3.13).

D. Fiduciary Activities: Judge must not serve as an executor, administrator, or other fiduciary, unless "close familial relationship." Must not get involved in matters likely to go to his or her own court. (Code of Judicial Conduct 3.8).

E. Do Not Act as Arbitrator or Practice Law if Full-Time Judge (Code of Judicial Conduct 3.9).

F. Do Not Accept Appointments Unless to Improve the Law (Code of Judicial Conduct 3.4).

G. Do Not Get Involved in Discriminatory Activities or Organizations (Code of Judicial Conduct 3.6).

II. POLITICAL ACTIVITY OF JUDGES WHEN RUNNING FOR OFFICE

A. Do Not Endorse Publicly (other than if same office under Code of Judicial Conduct 4.2) (Code of Judicial Conduct 4.1).

B. Be Honest and Not Misleading: Can take a position, in a dignified way, on even contested political issues, under the First Amendment Free Speech Clause. *Minnesota v. White* (2002). Note: This U.S. Supreme Court pronouncement supersedes the former code provision to the contrary. (Code of Judicial Conduct 2.10).

C. Do Not Solicit Funds: Let campaign committee handle all money and public support. (Code of Judicial Conduct 4.1 and 4.4).

D. Resignation: If running for non-judicial office. (Code of Judicial Conduct 4.5).

III. PERFORMING A JUDGE'S DUTIES IMPARTIALLY AND DILIGENTLY

A. Be Fair/Courteous to All in the Courtroom: Do not consider communications by others outside court re: the proceeding. Can get the advice of a disinterested expert if all parties are notified and given the chance to respond. (Code of Judicial Conduct 2.9).

B. Disqualify Self Where "Impartiality Might Reasonably Be Questioned" (due process violation): Disqualify if you know about the facts of case, know the lawyer, made a statement about the case when running for office, are related to lawyers or parties, etc. However, mere negative rulings do not meet this standard. (Code of Judicial Conduct 2.11).

Examples:

1. Bias, prejudice, personal knowledge of facts.
2. Served as lawyer. Know lawyer/s personally.
3. Judge, spouse or minor child living in judge's house has more than *de minimis* financial or any other interest that could be substantially affected by outcome.
4. Any close family member who is a party, witness, or lawyer in a case, judge has more than *de minimis* interest.

C. Do Not Commend/Criticize Jurors (Code of Judicial Conduct 2.8).

D. Do Not Make Unnecessary Appointments (Code of Judicial Conduct 2.13).

E. Do Whistle-Blowing on Judges, Lawyers (Code of Judicial Conduct 2.15).

Lesson 6
Dishonesty and Misconduct

I. LYING ON YOUR BAR APPLICATION AND MISCONDUCT

A. False Statements/Failure to Disclose Material Facts on Bar Application (Rule 8.1):

1. Rule 8.1 states: "An applicant for admission to the bar, or a lawyer in connection with a bar admission application or in connection with a disciplinary matter, shall not: (a) knowingly make a false statement of material fact; or (b) fail to disclose a fact necessary to correct a misapprehension known by the person to have arisen in the matter . . ."

2. One who lies on his or her bar application will be subject to discipline after passing the bar. However, good faith mistakes are permissible.

   a. Note re Discipline: Discipline is neither civil nor criminal. It is an administrative action undertaken by the state bar to protect the public from dangerously bad lawyers. Thus, only licensed attorneys are subject to discipline. First-time good faith mistakes probably will not subject the attorney to discipline. Rather, a pattern of violation is necessary.

B. General Misconduct: Duty of Honesty and Integrity (a "Catch-All") (Rule 8.4):

1. Public should be protected from those who are not qualified to be lawyers.

2. Crime or moral turpitude inside and outside lawyer's job.

3. Misconduct: A lawyer shall not:

    a. Violate the rules of professional conduct or knowingly assist or induce another in such violation.

    b. Engage in conduct involving moral turpitude. "Moral turpitude" can include any crime committed anywhere, i.e., a state can discipline its lawyers for misconduct committed outside the state. Moral turpitude also includes civil fraud.

    c. Engage in conduct prejudicial to the administration of justice.

    d. Engage in conduct that adversely reflects on fitness to practice law.

    e. State or imply that he or she has the ability to influence the government or a government official.

    f. Knowingly assist a judicial officer in violating the rules of judicial conduct or other law.

    g. Begin a new sexual relationship with client. (Rule 1.8(j)).

C. Reporting Ethical Violations ("Whistle-Blowing") (Rule 8.3):

1. General Rule: A lawyer who knows that another lawyer (or judge) has committed a violation that raises **a substantial question** of their ability to act as an attorney (or judge) **shall** inform the appropriate authority, unless the information is privileged.

D. Improving the Legal System:

1. Proper criticism of judicial system is permitted. (Rule 8.2) (Note: An attorney is subject to discipline for excessive criticism of judges.).

2. Lawyers should try to give at least 50 hours to pro bono work. (Rule 6.1).

3. A lawyer must not turn down appointed cases. (Rule 6.2).

4. Lawyers should work for law reform. (Rule 6.1).

E. Jurisdiction (Rule 8.5): A lawyer is subject to the disciplinary authority of the jurisdiction in which he or she is licensed even when engaged in practice elsewhere.

Lesson 7
Practicing Without a License

I. UNAUTHORIZED PRACTICE OF LAW

A. What Is the Practice of Law? Traditionally, understood to mean that work which requires a lawyer's skill and knowledge. (Rule 5.5). A lawyer is not allowed to practice law without being licensed in that state. Practicing law means:

1. Giving legal advice.
2. One must have a law license in that jurisdiction to practice law and/or represent others in court. (Trend: multi-jurisdictional practice allowed if an ABA school graduate, good standing, and 5 years of experience. You can apply for *pro hac vice* admission, which is temporary admission for that particular case).
3. Preparing documents: It is permissible for a lawyer to delegate work to non-licensed law clerks, secretaries, etc., provided that all work is adequately supervised by the attorney (Rule 5.3), and the attorney reads every document. The attorney is fully responsible for all such work.
4. Why is it important practically? If a lawyer or law firm "practices law" without being licensed in the state, the lawyer/law firm could lose any fees that it/they earned in that state. Note: you cannot work remotely in a state in which you are not licensed (other than a vacation).

B. Sharing Fees (Rule 5.4):

1. General rule: a lawyer must not share legal fees with a non-lawyer.
2. There are exceptions:
   a. An agreement by a lawyer with his firm, partner or associate may provide for the payment of money to one or more specified persons.

   b. Retirement plan or profit sharing.

3. Fee-sharing with non-lawyers is prohibited.

4. A lawyer shall not allow a non-lawyer to direct or control the professional judgment of a lawyer. (Rule 5.4).

5. Non-lawyers cannot own law firms, and a lawyer cannot form a partnership with any individual not licensed to practice law if any activities of that partnership will be the practice of law (but can do mutual non-compensated referrals to non-lawyers).

6. Reciprocal referral arrangements: A lawyer may receive referrals without a fee from other lawyers or (or other non-lawyers) in exchange for referring some of the lawyer's clients, but the arrangement cannot be exclusive and the clients must be aware of the arrangement. (Rule 7.2(b)(4)).

C. <u>Proper Identification and Permissive Advertising</u> (Rule 7.1):

   1. Phone, cards, door, letterhead. (Rule 7.1).

      A lawyer shall not use a firm name, letterhead or other professional designation that violates Rule 7.1. Rule 7.1 states that a lawyer shall not make a false or misleading statement.

   2. Failure to tell of suspended status.

   3. An attorney who is not a certified specialist may not advertise that she is a certified specialist. (Rule 7.4 requires that an attorney honestly advertise her field of specialization).

Lesson 8
Competence and Diligence

I. DISCIPLINE VS. MALPRACTICE

A. Competence Generally (Rule 1.1): **An affirmative duty to utilize the legal knowledge, skill, thoroughness, and preparation reasonably necessary for the representation**. Perfect competence is not required, but the lawyer must not be so incompetent that reasonable preparation would not bring him or her up to speed.

1. Ability to handle this matter properly: Lawyers are presumed competent, i.e., need not be an expert to take a case. Association with a more expert lawyer or study are both acceptable so as to gain "competence." Association with other counsel requires client's written consent. Emergency exception: held to a lower standard in an emergency; associate with competent counsel as soon as possible. (Rule 1.1).

B. Diligence and Promptness Required (Rule 1.3): A lawyer shall act with reasonable diligence and promptness in representing a client.

1. Communication (client abandonment cases):

   a. Keep client informed and promptly comply with reasonable requests for information. (Rule 1.4).

   b. Note: Supervisory lawyer is responsible vicariously for subordinate's incompetence under Rule 5.1.

   c. Settlement offers:

      1) Lawyers must communicate to their clients all offers of settlement made by opposing parties. (Rule 1.4, Comment 2). In class actions, communication to the class representative will suffice.

      2) A lawyer shall not accept compensation for representing a client from one other than the

client unless the lawyer obtains the client's informed written consent, provided that no disclosure or consent is required if such nondisclosure is otherwise authorized by law or the lawyer is rendering legal services on behalf of any public agency. (Rule 1.8(f)).

C. Special Roles and Fiduciary Responsibilities

1. Role of partner/supervising lawyer (Vicarious Liability): A partner is responsible for his associate's work, and must ensure that everyone complies with ethical rules. (Rule 5.1).
2. Role of subordinate lawyer: "Just followed orders" is no excuse. (Rule 5.2).
3. Responsibility for non-lawyers (bookkeeper cases) proper hiring, training, supervision. (Rule 5.3).
4. Prosecutor's role (Rule 3.8): Different duty: Minister of justice as well as advocate for the government:
   a. Must personally believe there is a likelihood of guilt and that belief must be reasonable; otherwise, must refrain from prosecuting.
   b. Make reasonable efforts to assure that the accused has been advised of the right to, and the procedure for, obtaining counsel.
   c. Refrain from getting waiver of pretrial rights from an unrepresented defendant.
   d. Make timely disclosure of evidence that tends to negate the guilt of the accused or mitigates the offense.
   e. Exercise reasonable care to prevent investigators, law enforcement personnel, etc. from making improper extrajudicial statements.
   f. Do not subpoena lawyer for testimony unless no alternative.

5. Malpractice and Limiting Liability:

   a. An agreement limiting malpractice liability is permissible *only if* the client is independently represented in making the agreement. (Rule 1.8(h)(1)). Typically called "prospectively" limiting liability and it can be against public policy.

Lesson 9
Trust Accounts

I. <u>AVOIDING IMPROPRIETY</u>

A. <u>Acceptance of Employment</u>: General Rule: Do not take cases merely to harass opponents (Civil Procedure—FRCP 11 Sanctions):

1. Judicial Capacity/Public Employee: Do not accept if prior substantial responsibility. (Rule 1.11).

2. Improper Influence: Lawyers must not claim or imply that they have the ability to exert any improper influence over any aspect of the legal system. (Rule 8.4).

B. <u>Identity of Trust Account Funds; Safekeeping Property</u> (Rule 1.15):

1. Notify, deposit, identify, keep records for five years, and render accounting on demand.

2. Account must be in same state as lawyer's office unless the client consents.

3. Trust accounts: Unnecessary if the attorney is on salary. However, if the attorney receives money that is part his or her own and part the client's, or receives an advancement of fees, it must be deposited in a trust account.

   a. **Commingling:** Not permitted. All money not owned by the lawyer must be kept in a trust account. All money owned by the lawyer must be kept out of the trust account.

   b. **Disputes/Claims:** If there is a dispute about the money, it should be left in the account and the attorney should suggest arbitration. If a third-party creditor makes a claim to the money, it should be left in the trust account until the matter is resolved.

c. Interest on lawyer trust accounts, "IOLTA," is a "taking" as under the Fifth and Fourteenth Amendments but does not offend the Constitution. *Brown v. Legal Foundation of Washington* (2003) 538 U.S. 216, 123 S. Ct. 1406, 155 L. Ed. 2d 376.

4. Holding Chattels: Chattel must be labeled and appropriately safeguarded.

C. Contact with Officials (Rule 3.5):

1. Do not give/lend anything of value to one connected with tribunal.

2. Generally, no *ex parte* communications with judge. If such communications occur, there will be no discipline if notice of the communication is given to the other party as soon as practicable.

D. Public Office Lawyers (Rule 1.11 and related Comments):

1. Shall not unfairly use position for him or herself or client.

2. Shall not use position to influence the tribunal.

3. Shall not accept gifts, etc., if given to influence the judgment.

4. However, surprisingly, prosecutors, provided all other due process rights are safeguarded, are permitted to execute a search warrant on an attorney while the attorney's client is before a grand jury. There is no per se violation of the attorney's due process rights, e.g., to earn a living. *Cunningham v. Hamilton County, Ohio* (1999) 527 U.S. 198, 119 S. Ct. 1915, 144 L. Ed. 2d 18.

Lesson 10
Advertising

I. FIRST AMENDMENT AND ADVERTISING

A. Advertising (Fraud; First Amendment—Commercial Speech issues):

1. Definition: General announcement to the general public regarding availability of legal services.

2. General Rule: Advertisements cannot be misleading. (Rule 7.1):

   a. No material misrepresentation of fact or law or omission of fact.

   b. Must not be likely to create unjustified expectation about results.

   c. Must not imply ability to achieve results by illegal means.

   d. Must not compare services with other lawyers (without ability to factually substantiate the comparison).

3. First Amendment Freedom of Speech/Fourteenth Amendment Due Process: Commercial Speech doctrine protects attorney advertising which is not misleading. Such speech can be restricted only if necessary to further a substantial government interest, and if the limitation is narrowly tailored to meet that interest. *Bates v. Arizona State Bar* (1977) 433 U.S. 350, 97 S. Ct. 2691, 53 L. Ed. 2d 81:

   a. Claims such as "very reasonable rates" are not necessarily "misleading."

   b. States cannot issue a "laundry list" of mandatory language for advertisements, e.g., it is unconstitutional to discipline an attorney for violating a state rule requiring the use of the word "torts" rather than words "personal injury." *In re R.M.J.* (1982) 455 U.S. 191, 102 S. Ct. 929, 71 L. Ed. 2d 64.

c. States cannot institute a blanket ban on print advertising oriented toward a particular legal problem or potential defendant. However, the attorney can be disciplined for not telling clients they will be responsible for fees and costs. *Zauderer v. Office of Disciplinary Counsel of the Supreme Court of Ohio* (1985) 471 U.S. 626, 105 S. Ct. 2265, 85 L. Ed. 2d 652.

d. States cannot discipline a lawyer for a reasonable communication of areas of expertise or, e.g., for a truthful advertisement that he or she is also an accountant. *Ibanez v. Florida Department of Business and Professional Regulation, Board of Accountancy* (1994) 512 U.S. 136, 114 S. Ct. 2084, 129 L. Ed. 2d 118.

4. Names of Firms and Letterhead (Rule 7.1)

   a. Any name is permissible if not misleading.

   b. Examples of "misleading":

      1) Falsely identifying the firm as a partnership when in fact the lawyers are only sharing an office.

      2) Implying affiliation with the government or charitable organization.

Lesson 11
Soliciting Clients

I. SOLICITATION (Rule 7.3)

1. Definition: Attorney-initiated contact with a specific individual regarding a known legal problem ("ambulance chasing").
2. General rule: Solicitation is prohibited, unless the solicited individual is a family member or there was a prior professional relationship. Solicitation is prohibited if it constitutes "coercion, duress or harassment" or if the recipient communicates a desire not to be solicited.
3. A lawyer who has given unsolicited advice to a layperson who needs a lawyer (or should take legal action) shall not accept employment resulting from that advice.

   Exceptions:

   1) Employment by close friend, relative, or former client.
   2) Employment resulting from participation in activities designed to educate laypersons.
   3) Employment resulting from a referral from a legal assistance organization that recommended the lawyer.
   4) Employment resulting from the joinder of others in a class action dependent on the joinder of those others.
   5) No fee whatsoever is taken.
4. "Direct contact with prospective client" is permissible where:

   a. Family or prior professional relationship.

b. Properly labeled ad ("Advertising Material" written on the envelope and at the beginning and ending of any recorded or electronic communication).

c. Prepaid legal service plan.

5. In-person or electronic solicitation: A state may forbid in-person or electronic solicitation for pecuniary gain. Rationale: the personal presence of a trained advocate has coercive force. *Ohralik v. Ohio Star Bar Association* (1978) 436 U.S. 447, 98 S. Ct. 1912, 56 L. Ed. 2d 444.

6. Group or prepaid legal plans are different: Such services are permitted to market their services by in-person or telephone contact so long as the persons contacted are not known to need legal services in a particular matter, and the lawyer does not own or direct the organization. Rationale: reduced chances for coercion since representative (not lawyer) is making the contact.

7. Direct-mail: States cannot completely ban targeted direct-mail advertising, e.g., letters to homeowners subject to foreclosure okay. Rationale: little or no invasion of privacy. *Shapero v. Kentucky Bar Association* (1988) 486 U.S. 466, 108 S. Ct. 1916, 100 L. Ed. 2d 475.

   a. State bars may keep lawyers from sending solicitations to accident victims for 30 days. *Florida Bar v. Went For It, Inc.* (1995) 515 U.S. 618, 115 S. Ct. 2371, 132 L. Ed. 2d 541.

8. Pro bono services: A lawyer cannot be disciplined for solicitation of pro bono (free) services unless the state proves attorney overreaching, fraud, or abuse. *In re Primus* (1978) 436 U.S. 412, 98 S. Ct. 1893, 56 L. Ed. 2d 417.

A. <u>Recommending Legal Assistance</u> (Rule 7.2)

1. General rule: The lawyer must not give "anything of value" to a person for recommending the lawyer's services.

2. Exceptions: Payments of reasonable advertising costs; Payments of usual charges for nonprofit referral services. (Note, however, that payments to public media in exchange for publicity are prohibited.)

Lesson 12
Attorney's Fees

I. REASONABLENESS OF ATTORNEY'S FEES

A. Fees (Rule 1.5): Most-testable issues are: (1) the amount of the fee; (2) division of fees between two or more lawyers; and (3) fee disputes:

1. Amount of the Fee: General Rule: Lawyers' fees must be "reasonable," accurate, well-communicated:

   a. Basic factors considered in the reasonableness analysis include the following:

      1) Time, labor, novelty, and skill required.

      2) Fee customarily charged for similar work in that locality.

      3) The amount of the fee and the results obtained.

      4) Time limitations imposed by client or the circumstances.

      5) Experience, reputation of lawyer.

      6) Nature/length of relationship with client.

      7) Whether the fee is fixed or contingent. *Example*: $100,000 for ten hours work may or may not be "unreasonable."

2. Contingent Fees. (Rule 1.5(d))

   a. Not permitted in domestic relations cases where the fee depends upon any of the following: (1) Securing a divorce; (2) The amount of alimony/support; (3) The amount of any property settlement in lieu of alimony or support. (Note: CAN receive contingency for ongoing collection, e.g., support). (Rule 1.5(d)(1)).

   b. Not permitted in criminal cases. (Rule 1.5(d)(2)).

c. Contingency fee agreement must be in writing and explained. The writing must explain the method by which the fee is calculated, including percentages payable upon settlement, what expenses will be deducted from the recovery. (Rule 1.5(c)).

3. Division of fees among lawyers not in same firm (not referral fees). (Rule 1.5(e)).

   a. Require client consent. The fee shall not be increased as a result of the division of labor, and should be proportional to the workload and responsibility of the lawyers involved.

      1) Gifts to referring lawyers are probably permissible so long as not offered or given in consideration of any agreement for future referrals.

4. Fee Disputes/Collection of Fees: If there is a dispute about the attorney's fees, the disputed funds should be left in the trust account. You cannot bring a claim against your client until the matter has been resolved. If a third-party creditor makes a claim to the money, it should be left in the trust account. (Rule 1.15):

   a. Lawyer can reveal client confidences for purposes of resolving fee disputes. (Rule 1.6).

   b. Arbitration: Lawyer must offer arbitration if there's a fee dispute. (Rule 1.5, Comment 9).

Lesson 13
Limitations on Right to Practice

I. RESTRICTIONS ON THE RIGHT TO PRACTICE LAW

A. Non-Compete Clauses and the Sale of a Law Practice:

1. A lawyer cannot participate in offering or making a partnership or employment agreement that restricts the rights of a lawyer to practice after termination of the relationship—except regarding retirement benefits. (Rule 5.6).
2. Non-Competition Clauses: prohibited. (Rule 5.6(a)).
3. Settlement Agreements: A lawyer must not participate in the offering or making of an agreement in which a restriction on a lawyer's right to practice is part of the settlement of a controversy. (Rule 5.6(b)).
4. Can sell law practice, provided 90-day notice is given to each (former) client that they can choose a new lawyer. (Rule 1.17).

Lesson 14
Conflicts of Interest: Concurrent

I. AN ATTORNEY CANNOT TAKE ON A CASE WHERE THE ATTORNEY WILL BE SUBSTANTIALLY LIMITED

A. General Rule: An attorney must not take cases to harass or annoy the opposing party. (Rule 3.1). An attorney must avoid conflicts of interest. (Rule 1.7).

B. Conflicts of Interest (Rule 1.7)

1. Actual vs. Potential:

   a. Actual: An attorney must not take a case that poses an actual conflict of interest.

   b. Potential: If there is only a mere potential for conflict, the attorney can take the case if he or she fully discloses that potential to the client.

      1) The potential conflict must be waived by informed consent, in writing. (Rule 1.7).

      2) *Caveat*: If (at any point), an actual conflict develops, the attorney must withdraw (see also "Multiple Representation," below).

2. Waiver of Conflicts ("Consent") Generally: Clients can waive "potential" conflicts but not "actual" conflicts.

   a. Client can consent ("waive") if the lawyer has a reasonable belief the client will not be adversely affected by the representation and the client makes a knowing, written waiver. When a disinterested lawyer would conclude that the client should not agree to the representation under the circumstances, the lawyer can neither ask for consent nor provide representation based on the client's consent.

b. Note that these general principles are modified depending on the "type" of conflict, as discussed below.

3. Types of Conflicts:

a. Conflicts of interest between the client and the lawyer. (Rule 1.7). A lawyer must not represent a client if the representation of that client may be *materially limited* by the lawyer's own interests, unless the lawyer reasonably believes there will be no adverse effect, and the client consents after consultation, in writing.

1) Personal: The attorney's own personal interests should never be permitted to outweigh the interests of the client. A lawyer must not use the client's confidences for the advantage of the lawyer or a 3rd person (unless there is consent after full disclosure), whether or not it disadvantages the client.

2) Personal relationship: No new sexual relationship with client. (Rule 1.8).

3) Financial/Business relations: An attorney cannot enter business deal with a client where the deal is somehow adverse to the interests of the client. Mere informed consent is insufficient; there must be general fairness.

a) Writing required.

b) Gifts: An attorney must not prepare a document that gives himself or herself a gift, unless the document is a will prepared for a relative.

c) Book rights: An attorney must not get book rights to a trial before it is over.

d) Loans/Interest-free advances:

(1) If the advance is simply costs and fees, it is acceptable in all jurisdictions. In a majority, repayment of such can be

contingent on the positive outcome. (Rule 1.8). In a minority, the client must repay such regardless of outcome.

(2) If the "advance" is a loan, it is illegal in almost all states.

b. Conflicts of interest between the client and third parties (also called "concurrent" conflict of interest).

1) Rule 1.7(b): A lawyer shall not represent a client if the representation of that client may be materially limited by the lawyer's responsibilities to another client or to a third person unless:

a) The lawyer reasonably believes the representation will not be adversely affected;

b) The client consents after consultation; and

c) There is a writing affirming consent

d) Potential Conflict: Third-Party Payment. Legal services paid for by third parties: Third party payment is permissible if the client consents. (Rule 1.8(f)).

i. Duty of loyalty is owed to the client, not the payor.

Lesson 15
Conflicts of Interest: Corporations

I. CORPORATIONS (Rule 1.13)

A. The corporation is the client (not its employees or officers).

B. When a lawyer knows an officer or employee of the corporation will engage in improper behavior, the lawyer should act in the best interests of the corporation depending on the seriousness of the potential damage to the corporation.

C. The lawyer should advise each employee of the corporation to consult with independent counsel.

D. If the lawyer knows that an officer or employee of the corporation is engaged in harmful actions toward the corporation, then the lawyer can proceed as is necessary in the best interest of the organization. (Rule 1.13). Further, the lawyer shall refer the matter to a higher authority in the organization if no one is responding to the lawyer's concerns.

   1. If even after referral, the highest authority (usually the Board of Directors) fails to act or refuses to act, and the lawyer believes that the corporation will be harmed, then the lawyer may reveal information relating to the representation even though confidentiality concerns (Rule 1.6) may typically prohibit such disclosure. The lawyer is allowed to do what is necessary to prevent substantial injury to the organization. (Rule 1.13).

   2. However, the lawyer may not whistle-blow with respect to information relating to a lawyer's representation of an organization. (Rule 1.13).

E. When a conflict arises with an officer (or other employee), the attorney must immediately explain that he or she is the attorney of the corporation and not the officer or employee.

F. It is acceptable for the lawyer to represent the corporation and officer with permission from the corporation granted by an officer other than the one receiving the representation.

Lesson 16
Conflicts of Interest: Former Clients and Imputation

I. CONFLICTS OF INTEREST BETWEEN CLIENTS

A. Former Clients: A lawyer who has formerly represented a client shall not thereafter represent another person in the *same or a substantially related matter* in which that person's interests are adverse to the interests of the former client. (Rule 1.9).

B. Multiple Representation/Simultaneous Clients: (6th Amendment Right to Counsel): Lawyers "should" try to avoid multiple representation.

1. Rule 1.7: Attorneys must not represent a client if the representation of that client will be adverse to another client, unless: (1) the attorney reasonably believes there will be no adverse effect on the relationship with the other client; and (2) the client consents after consultation, i.e., "waiver," in writing.
2. Divided loyalty: A lawyer must not take a client if his loyalty is divided. Although it is permissible to take multiple clients, if an "actual" conflict of interest develops, the lawyer must withdraw from all of them. (Rule 1.7).
3. To accept multiple plaintiffs or multiple defendants in civil or criminal cases, each client must consent after disclosure, with written affirmation. The disclosure must advise the client that multiple-representation may not be best for her interests.
4. Note: Aggregate settlement offers: If an aggregate settlement offer is made to multiple clients, the lawyer cannot accept the offer on behalf of the clients unless all of them agree on how to divide it. (Rule 1.8(g)).

II. IMPUTED DISQUALIFICATION: WHEN A LAWYER CHANGES JOBS (Rule 1.10)

A. When a lawyer changes firms, his or her new firm is disqualified from taking cases against the former clients if he or she acquired confidential information about those clients. The lawyers in the new firm are vicariously disqualified, i.e., disqualification is "imputed" to the whole firm, because every lawyer is deemed to "know everything" about every case the firm has.

Exceptions:

a. If one of the vicariously disqualified lawyers leaves the firm and joins another, his or her new firm is not necessarily disqualified.

b. Waiver by opposing party.

c. Former government lawyers in private practice.

1) Rule 1.11 provides that a lawyer who has worked personally and substantially on a matter while working for the government shall not represent that matter in private practice.

2) The firm may take steps to prevent the conflict from becoming imputed to all other attorneys. The firm in this situation can prevent imputation by screening the ex-government attorney from the matter, not sharing any fees from the matter with that attorney, and notifying the government of the possible conflict of interest so that the government can ensure that proper preventative measures are taken.

B. Note: Lawyers who share office space and occasionally consult each other will be regarded as a "firm" if they present themselves to the public in a way that suggests they are a firm.

C. Related Lawyers (Rule 1.8): A lawyer may be disqualified from representing a client if that lawyer's relative is also a lawyer and represents a person with interests directly adverse to the first lawyer's client (however, the firm is not disqualified if there is adequate screening).

D. Testimony of Lawyer/Firm:

1. Lawyer cannot be witness. One cannot be the lawyer on a case in which he or she is to be a witness on a contested issue (conflict created). However, it is permissible for the attorney to take the stand for uncontested issues, attorney fees, and if there would be a substantial hardship on the client. (Rule 3.7).

Lesson 17
The Attorney-Client Relationship and Duty of Confidentiality

I. THE SCOPE OF RELATIONSHIP BETWEEN ATTORNEY AND CLIENT

A. Client Decisions: The client has final authority over the big "structural decisions," i.e., whether or not to settle, what plea to enter, whether or not to take the case to trial, whether or not to demand trial by jury, whether to appeal, etc. (Rule 1.2).

B. Attorney Decisions: The attorney has decision-making authority over legal strategies and tactics, e.g., what witnesses to call and what order to call them in. (Rule 1.2).

C. Limits on Objectives of Representation: A lawyer may limit the objectives of the representation if the client consents after consultation. (Rule 1.2). This is called a limited-scope representation.

D. Advisor: Lawyers have a duty to exercise independent professional judgment and render candid advice, which may include moral, economical, and political considerations. (Rule 2.1).

II. DUTY OF CONFIDENTIALITY

A. General Rule: Keep it to yourself forever. Communications between the attorney and client for purposes of representation are protected. (Rule 1.6):

1. This duty survives even the death of the client. *Swindler & Berlin v. United States* (1998) 524 U.S. 399, 118 S. Ct. 2081, 141 L. Ed. 2d 379.

B. Client Confidences:

1. "Smoking guns" and other evidence: Look, don't touch. (Rule 3.4). Rule 3.4 requires fairness in dealing with

opposing party which requires that a lawyer not alter evidence or hide evidence:

a. The protection of attorney-client confidences ceases when tangible evidence is in the possession of the attorney, or when the attorney interferes with material evidence.

b. If the attorney does not possess the item of evidence or interfere with it, he or she is precluded from revealing any information about it.

2. Rule 1.6

a. Definition (Broad): All information about a client relating to the representation.

b. Disclosure by lawyer; **prohibited unless:**

1) Client consents.

2) Disclosure is *impliedly authorized* in order to carry out the representation.

3) Lawyer reasonably believes disclosure is necessary to prevent criminal acts which the lawyer believes will result in death or substantial bodily harm or substantial financial injury (must be reasonably certain).

4) Lawyer reasonably believes disclosure is necessary regarding a dispute between the lawyer and the client.

5) Information gained in the professional relationship that the client has requested be kept secret, or that which would be embarrassing or would be likely to be detrimental to the client is also protected, but is NOT protected by the attorney-client evidentiary privilege, i.e., if subpoenaed the attorney must reveal the "embarrassing secret."

6) Lawyer must rectify likely perjury during pendency of case. (Rule 3.3).

Caveat: The duty of confidentiality protects any disclosure of all information given by a potential client to an attorney relating to the representation of the client, regardless of when or where it was acquired, and non-interfering observations (look, do not touch), which are the fruit of the client's communications. It also covers testimonial evidence. For example, the client tells attorney enough facts that the attorney will look for the chattel. It is much broader than the evidentiary attorney-client privilege.

The attorney-client relationship begins when the client reasonably believes that the attorney is an attorney and seeks legal advice.

C. Effect of Sale of Law Practice (Rule 1.17)

1. It is permissible to sell a law practice, but entire practice or area of practice must be sold. Seller must cease to practice in the practice area sold, within the geographical area of the practice. Seller must give 90-day notice to each of his or her clients and obtain client consent before revealing confidences to the purchaser.
2. Note: Purchaser can raise rates reasonably, but the purchase must not be financed by increases in fees.

Lesson 18
Zealous Representation

I. MERITORIOUS CLAIMS AND CANDOR

A. General Rule: Meritorious, speedy, candid, fair. (Rule 1.3).

B. Respect for Rights of Third Persons: Lawyers must not act for the mere purpose to harass, delay or burden a third person. (Rule 4.4).

Inadvertent Disclosure. (Rule 4.4(b)). A lawyer who receives a document (email or fax) relating to the representation of the lawyer's client and knows, or reasonably should know, that the document was inadvertently sent shall promptly notify the sender so the sender can take protective measures.

C. Meritorious Claims and Contentions:

1. No "frivolous" proceedings or defenses (but a lawyer for a defendant in a criminal proceeding may defend the proceeding so as to require that every element of the case be established) unless there is a good faith argument for a change in the law. (Rule 3.1). Note: Subject to "Rule 11" civil sanctions if frivolous (objective standard).

2. Must make reasonable efforts to expedite litigation within the client's interests. (Rule 3.2).

D. Fairness to Opposing Party (Rule 3.4)

1. Lawyers must not obstruct another party's access to evidence.

2. Lawyers must not ask persons other than their clients or relatives to refrain from giving relevant information to another party.

E. Perjured/False Evidence: Lawyers must not falsify evidence or counsel a witness to testify falsely. (Rule 3.4). Must rectify likely perjury within pendency of case. (Rule 3.3). If a lawyer knows that the defendant wants to testify falsely, the lawyer must try to convince the defendant not to do so or may ask the court to withdraw. As a last resort, the lawyer must disclose enough information to the court to set the matter straight.

F. Truthfulness in Statements to Others: Lawyers must not make false statements of fact or law to a third person or fail to disclose a material fact when necessary to avoid assisting a crime or fraud by a client (unless the information is privileged, as discussed above in "Confidences"). (Rule 4.1).

G. Candor Toward Tribunal (Rule 3.3)

1. A lawyer must not create or offer false evidence and must take remedial measures during pendency of case if he or she comes to learn that the offered evidence was false.

2. A lawyer must not knowingly fail to disclose legal authority contrary to his or her client's position and not disclosed by opposing counsel.

H. Illegal Acts

1. Lawyers must not counsel/assist client in an illegal act. (Rules 1.2(d); 3.3(b)).

2. Lawyers must not engage in illegal conduct or violate the rules of professional conduct. (Rule 8.4).

I. Undue Influence: Lawyers must not exercise undue influence over client for the lawyer's advantage.

J. Client Commits Fraud on Person/Tribunal During Representation

1. Lawyer must take remedial measures and then withdraw if necessary, during trial and appeals of right. (Rule 3.3).

2. If person other than client, lawyer must immediately reveal to tribunal.

3. Fraud not during course of representation: Keep confidential.

K. Threatening Criminal Charges to Gain Advantage in a Civil Case

1. Model Rules prohibit, but *contra* ABA Formal Op. 92–363 (1992)—may be proper to mention the potential of criminal complaint that is related to civil action.

L. Transactions with Persons Other than Clients

1. Unless their attorney or the Court approves, do not communicate, directly or indirectly, with represented party. (Rule 4.2).
2. Can advise to get counsel.
3. A lawyer who deals with an unrepresented person as part of representation of a client must disclose to the unrepresented person that she is a lawyer.

Lesson 19
Candor Toward the Tribunal

I. TRIAL CONDUCT: RESPECT FOR THE TRIBUNAL (Rule 3.5)

A. Follow Court Rules: Can in good faith challenge (no act intended to disrupt).

B. Be honest, fair, courteous.

C. Leave out personal opinions/facts.

D. Contact with jurors: Lawyers must avoid actual and potential contact with jurors. If the lawyer has contact, he or she must tell the judge. However, it is permissible to poll the jurors after the trial.

E. Opposing party must be notified if the attorney has an *ex parte* contact with the judge.

F. Witnesses: No contingent fees, but can pay reasonable expenses (Rule 3.4).

II. PUBLICITY (CRIMINAL AND CIVIL) (Rule 3.6)

A. *General rule*: Lawyers must not make extrajudicial statements likely to prejudice the proceedings, e.g., talking about the identity of witnesses, the reputation of the accused, etc. Inadmissible evidence should not be discussed in pre-trial or trial publicity.

B. What you can say:

1. General nature of a claim or defense
2. Information in public record
3. Investigation in progress
4. Result of any step in the litigation
5. Request for assistance regarding evidence or information
6. Warning about person if dangerous

7. Rebut other side's public statements

C. Balance the right to a fair trial against the right to freedom of speech.

Lesson 20
Termination of the Attorney/ Client Relationship

I. ENDING THE ATTORNEY/CLIENT RELATIONSHIP

A. Mandatory Withdrawal (Rule 1.16(a))

1. If continuing the representation would violate any law or the Model Rules.
2. Lawyer's incapacity: Physical/mental/substance abuse.
3. Client's choice (fired) or client attempts to harass/injure another.
    a. Fees for fired lawyers
        1) Lawyers cannot sue for wrongful termination, only for *quantum meruit* of services rendered.
        2) Contingent fee cases: Fired attorney does not receive the contingent fee.
            a) Case ultimately loses: If no money is ultimately received on the case, fired attorney only receives costs, e.g., filing fees, etc.
            b) Case ultimately wins: Fired attorney receives only the *quantum meruit* of his or her services. Depending on the circumstances, the *quantum meruit* may be the attorney's hourly rate or more (but rarely the full contingency fees).

B. Permissive Withdrawal (Rule 1.16(b))

1. Client uncooperative, unreasonable, or attempting illegal conduct.
    a. Failure to fulfill obligations to lawyer with prior warning.
    b. Pursuing improper objective.

2. Hardship on attorney.
3. Must have no material adverse effect on the client.

C. Procedural Requirements:

1. Promptly turn over files.
2. Refund unearned fees promptly.
3. Judicial approval, if attorney has made an appearance in front of court.
4. Attorney must continue to honor client confidentiality.

CHAPTER 5

SIMULATED MPRE EXAMS

In the materials following this page, there are two simulated MPRE full exams. After each full question set, a series of answer explanations follows. It is very important for you not only to score yourself, but also to review the answer explanations in detail. This process is where a great deal of learning comes into play! If you only look at the correct answer and then move on, you are losing the best opportunity for you to learn from the simulated exams.

You should time yourself *loosely* for the first exam—note where you are in the questions after the first hour and then where you are after the second hour. Don't worry about the time as much as going through the questions thoroughly. If you don't know an answer, choose one anyway and know to come back. By choosing an answer, you protect yourself from giving away points.

For the second simulated MPRE, pay more attention to time. Make sure that after the first hour you are at least 1/2 way done; if not, pretend you are in the exam and work on strategies for how to make up time so you can move through the questions a little faster. One key strategy is to always read the "call" of the question first. You can move through the fact patterns more quickly if you know what topic the question involves.

Know that if you feel it's an easier question, you can answer quickly. There will be a certain percentage of easy questions, medium questions, and difficult questions. If you get an easy question and know the answer, take advantage and move quickly!

Think also about how you will deal with a time crunch. It is not likely to happen, but if you do panic, it's helpful to have a plan to move through the last 10 questions quickly. One important consideration: even if you have to guess the last few questions, do that instead of not finishing the exam. Remember, you are not penalized for wrong answers—so answer everything!

On the morning of the exam, take your rule book and skim through the rules again. You will always catch more information and substance by simply reviewing the rules. And remember, this is a test of minimum competency. You've trained well and you've got this!

Good luck!

MPRE Simulated Exam 1

Instructions:

You have 120 minutes to complete the following 60 questions. Please choose the best answer.

1. Paula and Donald are next-door neighbors and bitter personal enemies. Paula is suing Donald for trespass. Both parties believe in good faith in the correctness of their legal positions. Paula is represented by Lawyer Lucy and Donald is represented by Attorney Alexis. At the beginning of the representation, Paula told Lucy: "I don't want you to grant any delays or courtesies to Donald or his Lawyer. This is war, and I want you to insist on every technicality." Lucy has served written interrogatories on Donald. Due to a death in Donald's family, he has requested a one-week extension of the deadline for answering the interrogatories. May Lucy grant the extension?

   A. Yes, unless granting the extension would prejudice Paula's rights.

   B. Yes, because Alexis was not at fault in causing the delay.

   C. No, because Lucy owes a duty of loyalty to Paula.

   D. No, unless Paula changes her instructions and agrees to the extension.

2. Attorney Alfred is in-house legal counsel for the environmental group Save Our Scenery (SOS). SOS is opposed to a proposed shopping center development that would require the clearing of 500 acres of forest in Omega County. SOS has sponsored proposed legislation that would designate the forest as a State Park and prevent the development. However, the legislation is stuck in a legislative committee. In the meantime, the Omega County Council approved the proposed development by a unanimous voice vote. One of SOS's staff members brings to Alfred's attention a rule that requires a secret ballot vote in

all County Council matters. Alfred considers a lawsuit seeking to compel the Council to redo its earlier vote using a secret ballot. Though Alfred is certain that the result of a new vote would be the same, a "do over" would give the State Park legislation a chance to make it out of committee and be enacted. May Alfred file the lawsuit?

A. No, because the difference between a voice vote and a secret ballot vote is frivolous.

B. No, because Alfred's primary purpose in filing the suit would be delay.

C. Yes, because protecting the environment is a proper purpose.

D. Yes, because there is a valid legal basis for the lawsuit.

3. Millionaire actress Lana Larson dies unexpectedly of a drug overdose, leaving her entire fortune to her infant daughter Beatrice. Lana was married to Defendant Daniel at the time Beatrice was born. Under applicable law, Daniel is presumed to be Beatrice's father, but that presumption can be rebutted by a DNA test ordered pursuant to a parentage case. Plaintiff Patrick has come forward and claimed a long-time affair with Larson, and that he is Beatrice's father. Beatrice's father will exercise control over the child's now substantial fortune. Plaintiff Patrick has hired Attorney Alice to file a paternity action on his behalf. The matter has attracted substantial media attention, and as soon as Alice files the action, Attorney Alice is surrounded by reporters seeking a comment. Which of the following statements, if believed by Alice to be true, would be proper for her to make?

I. "As stated in our pleadings, we believe that a DNA test will prove conclusively that Patrick is the father of Beatrice."

II. "Lana was no longer in love with Daniel by the time Beatrice was conceived."

III. "We have been unable to locate several people whose testimony will be helpful to us, and we implore them to contact us immediately."

A. II only.

B. III only.

C. I and III, but not II.

D. I, II, and III.

4. Calico Corporation hires Attorney Albert to defend it in a products liability lawsuit. Calico's General Counsel, Gary, becomes dissatisfied with Albert's handling of the case, so he fires Albert and hires Lawyer Lois to continue the representation. While reviewing the file, Lois notices billing statements from Albert to Calico which reflect outrageously excessive charges for things like photocopying, travel expenses, and meals. When Lois asks Gary about the charges, Gary makes the following statement: "Look, I realize we made a mistake in hiring Albert. But we didn't pay those charges, and we're done with Albert, so I'd appreciate it if you would not pursue those charges any further." Is Lois subject to discipline if she fails to report her knowledge of Albert's overcharges to bar authorities?

A. No, unless Gary changes his mind and allows Lois to report the wrongdoing.

B. No, if Gary is convinced Calico was not harmed by the overcharges.

C. Yes, unless Lois believes the overcharges were a mistake.

D. Yes, if Lois believes Albert was guilty of professional misconduct.

5. A lawyer places an advertisement in a raunchy magazine. In the ad, he states that he has never lost a drunken driving case. The lawyer is subject to discipline because:

A. Advertising is per se unlawful.

B. Advertising is per se in violation of the rules.

C. The ad must be in a dignified forum.

D. The ad is misleading.

6. Many years ago, in college, a woman was suspended for being caught with a small amount of marijuana on her person. She was suspended for one semester, then later

returned to graduate with honors. On her bar application, she is asked if she was ever suspended from any school. She writes "no." Five years after being admitted, a former boyfriend of hers informs the bar. The bar investigates and finds that she knowingly lied. The lawyer is suspended from practice for 6 months. Is the suspension lawful?

A. No, because of the statute of limitations.

B. No, because it is unrelated to present moral turpitude.

C. Yes, because it is a very clear violation of the rules.

D. None of the above.

7. A lawyer learns that his boss, who is also an attorney, is embezzling funds. Because the lawyer fears for his job, he does nothing. The lawyer's silence is:

   A. Proper.

   B. Proper if he asks the boss to do the right thing and turn himself in.

   C. In violation of the rules of professional responsibility.

   D. In good faith, thus, excusable.

8. A lawyer goes on a hunting trip to Canada. One evening, he gets in a bar room brawl and kills two men. He is convicted of two counts of involuntary manslaughter. The lawyer's home state decides to discipline him. Is this permissible?

   A. No, because it was outside the state.

   B. No, because it was outside the country.

   C. No, because the actions were unrelated to the practice of law.

   D. Yes.

9. A man is on trial for willful tax fraud. His old friend, who is a municipal judge, knows that the man is of the highest moral character. The man could really use the judge's testimony, but only as it relates to the man's good character. Should the judge so testify?

   A. No, because it appears improper.

B. No, because judges can never be witnesses.

C. No, because the man may be of bad character.

D. Yes.

10. Attorney represented Plaintiff, who agreed to a settlement of $25,000. Attorney received a check in that amount from Defendant, payable to Attorney's order. Attorney endorsed and deposited the check in Attorney's Clients' Trust Account. Attorney promptly notified Plaintiff and billed Plaintiff $5,000 for legal fees. Plaintiff disputed the amount of the fee and wrote Attorney stating, "I will agree to pay $3,000 as a reasonable fee for the work you did, but I will not pay anything more than that." It is proper for Attorney to:

I. Send $20,000 to Plaintiff and retain $5000 in Attorney's Clients' Trust Account until the fee dispute is settled.

II. Send Plaintiff $20,000, transfer $3,000 to Attorney's office account, and retain $2,000 in Attorney's Clients' Trust Account until the dispute is settled.

III. Send Plaintiff $20,000 and transfer $5,000 to Attorney's office account.

A. I only.

B. II only.

C. I and II, but not III.

D. I, II, and III.

11. A state appellate judge teaches law for a local law school and is paid for her teaching. Which of the following are true?

A. She should not be paid, but since she is paid, she should report her income.

B. She should not be paid at all.

C. She should report her income.

D. She should not be teaching law.

12. A judge invests in the stock market for herself and her immediate family. She does quite well. Is this permissible?

A. Yes, because she does well.

B. Yes, because judges can do anything they want.

C. Yes, because a judge can manage her own finances.

D. Yes, because this business is unrelated to the practice of law.

13. Defendant Danny hires Lawyer Lucy to represent him in a driving under the influence (DUI) of alcohol case. They agree in a written retainer agreement that Lucy will be paid $200 per hour for her work. Unbeknownst to Danny, Lucy begins work on researching, writing, and filing an innovative motion to keep the results of the breathalyzer test Danny took out of evidence. The motion is ultimately successful, and the charges against Danny are dropped. However, as a result of the motion, Lucy bills Danny for approximately 100 more hours, or $20,000, more than an attorney would typically charge for a DUI defense.

Is Lucy subject to discipline?

A. No, because Danny was ultimately exonerated.

B. No, because $200 is a reasonable hourly fee.

C. Yes, unless Lucy really worked for all of the extra 100 hours for which she billed Danny.

D. Yes, because the fee charged was significantly more than other lawyers in the jurisdiction would have charged and Danny did not approve the additional fees in advance.

14. A lawyer is campaigning for judicial office. It is a tough race. The lawyer therefore pledges that, "If there is any doubt, I will order the maximum sentence." Is this proper?

A. Yes.

B. No.

C. More facts are needed.

D. It depends on the jurisdiction.

15. A lawyer has just passed and been admitted to the bar, after having failed it three times before. He decides to set up his own criminal law practice, even though he has virtually no

experience in this area. When he opens up a law office immediately after being admitted to the bar, he is:

A. Subject to discipline because he is per se incompetent in this legal area.

B. Subject to discipline because he is actually incompetent in this area.

C. Not subject to discipline because he is presumed competent.

D. Not subject to discipline because he is actually competent.

16. Lawyer Louis is one of the top communications lawyers in the country. The federal government announces that a limited number of new broadcast licenses will be made available next year. Two major broadcasting companies, CNNC and KBCJ, separately contact Louis and ask him to represent them in their applications for one of the new licenses. Though in some sense, the two companies will be competing for one of the limited number of licenses, Louis is confident that he can adequately represent each in their applications. May Louis represent both companies?

A. Yes, as long as each gives informed written consent and agrees to waive any actual and potential conflicts that may arise from the representation.

B. Yes, provided that each agrees to waive their right of confidentiality owed to them by Louis.

C. No, because the companies' interests are directly adverse in relation to obtaining a license.

D. No, because a lawyer owes each of his clients a duty of loyalty.

17. A lawyer represents a client who is charged with the statutory offense of "Driving an Automobile while under the Influence of Alcohol." The client talks with a slight lisp and tends to be snide when he is questioned. The lawyer, therefore, decides that the client must not take the stand in his own defense. The client insists that he be so allowed. The trial ends with the client fully acquitted, even though he did

not take the stand. Should the lawyer have let the client take the stand?

A. Yes, because this is an area of client decision.

B. Yes, because a client's fundamental desires should always be followed.

C. Yes, because the jury might have drawn an adverse conclusion from the client's silence.

D. No, because this was an area of attorney strategy.

18. A client is on trial for murder. He has pled not guilty. However, before trial, the client admits to the lawyer that he actually did commit the crime of which he was accused. If the lawyer coaches the client as to how best to lie on the stand, the lawyer is:

A. Behaving within the norms of the profession.

B. In technical violation of the norms, but not subject to discipline.

C. Subject to discipline.

D. Not subject to discipline.

19. A lawyer charges only $25 to prepare simple bankruptcy papers, intentionally undercutting the price of his peer lawyers. The lawyer's undercutting the price of his peer lawyers is:

A. In technical violation of the disciplinary norms.

B. In substantial violation of the norms.

C. Proper.

D. Improper.

20. A probate attorney prepares several wills for a client. Two weeks after preparing the last of such wills for that client, the client's sole beneficiary died. The attorney has found out about the death of the sole beneficiary. However, the attorney has not made subsequent contact with the client.

Which of the following is true?

A. It is improper for the attorney to contact the client; the attorney must wait for the client to contact him first.

B. It is proper for the attorney to contact the client regarding changing the will, and the attorney should, in fact, make such contact.

C. The attorney will be disciplined for his failure to contact the client.

D. None of the above.

21. A client comes to see a lawyer about a drunk driving case. The lawyer determines that this is a routine case and charges $10,000 to represent the client. This fee:

A. May be excessive and, thus, subjects her to possible discipline.

B. Is probably not excessive and, thus, is proper.

C. Is totally within her own discretion.

D. Is improper.

22. An attorney is contacted by the State Bar for potential discipline for charging "excessive fees." In order to discipline the attorney for charging an excessive fee, which of the following are relevant:

A. Her expertise, her reputation, and the difficulty of the case.

B. The difficulty of the case and the fees charged by similarly situated attorneys.

C. The attorney's expertise, her reputation, the difficulty of the case, and the fees charged by similarly situated attorneys.

D. The attorney's expertise, her reputation, the difficulty of the case, the fees charged by similarly situated attorneys, and the fees charged by one of the attorney's direct competitors.

23. Plaintiff Patty is suing her former employer Evenco for wrongful termination. On cross-examination, Evenco's lawyer asks Patty if she ever came to work under the influence of alcohol after March 31, 2009, a date upon which the parties agree Patty came to work drunk. Patty answers no. While the answer is literally true, Patty's lawyer Lucas

knows that Patty in fact went to work under the influence of a number of other narcotics besides alcohol on dates after March 31, 2009. Must Lucas disclose to the tribunal the fact that Patty appeared for work under the influence of narcotics after March 31, 2009?

A. No, because an attorney owes a paramount duty of confidentiality to their client.

B. No, because Patty's testimony was literally true.

C. Yes, because an attorney owes a duty of candor to the tribunal.

D. Yes, because an attorney must take remedial measures if the attorney reasonably believes the tribunal will draw a false inference from the evidence presented.

24. An attorney in a large law firm is contacted by a woman who wants that attorney to represent her in her divorce case. The attorney's firm charges a minimum of $20,000 to handle divorce cases. The woman cannot afford to pay more than $5,000. The attorney already does a great deal of pro bono work and, therefore, decides to refuse to represent the woman for less than $20,000. The attorney's refusal to represent the woman:

A. Is proper, because attorneys are rarely required to accept clients.

B. Is improper, because attorneys are not permitted to turn away clients in need.

C. Is improper, because $20,000 is an excessive fee.

D. Is proper, because the woman should not have contacted a large law firm to handle her case for only $5,000.

25. On one occasion, a client sought the services of an attorney for a criminal matter. The attorney refused to represent the client because the client could not afford the attorney's retainer. Finally, the attorney agreed to lower the retainer to just $2,000. However, the client told the attorney that he could not afford even a $2,000 retainer. The attorney felt sorry for the client and agreed to represent him "for $500 now, and you can pay me $1,500 if you are acquitted." The

client lost the case and was sent to prison. The attorney did not bill him for the $1,500.

The attorney's fee agreement with the client:

A. Was in good faith. Thus, the attorney is not subject to discipline.

B. Is a violation of the ethical norms, only if the attorney acted in good faith.

C. Is a violation of the rules, under the *Leon* case.

D. Subjects the attorney to discipline.

26. A transactional attorney charges different fees for clients, depending on the difficulty of the transaction. He also charges some clients with virtually identical cases different fees. Is this proper?

A. Yes, because attorneys do not need to bill the same amounts.

B. No because although different attorneys can bill different amounts to different clients, each individual attorney must bill the same amount to every client who has similar legal work. It is also a violation of the Equal Protection Clause.

C. No, because although different attorneys can bill different amounts to different clients, each individual attorney must bill the same amount to every client who has similar legal work.

D. No because it is a violation of the Equal Protection Clause.

27. A client seeks the advice of an attorney regarding highly complex litigation. The attorney calls a lawyer friend to see if he is willing to help out. The lawyer agrees, as does the client. The fee is not raised and the client agrees to this arrangement in writing. The attorney and the lawyer spend equal time on the client's case and split the fee equally.

Based on the above facts, is the attorney subject to discipline for utilizing the lawyer friend's services on this case?

A. Yes, because fee splits with attorneys outside the firm are per se violations of the norms of the profession.

B. Yes, because the fee split was not in proportion to the actual work performed.

C. Yes, because the client did not consent to the fee split.

D. No.

28. One attorney decides to associate with an attorney from another firm to assist him with a client's case. He obtains the client's consent, but fails to tell the client that she has the option to contact another attorney before consenting. The attorney and the associated attorney do equal work and split the fee equally. With regard to the fee split, it would have been preferable for the first attorney:

A. To have asked the client's permission prior to even calling the second attorney.

B. To have asked the client's permission prior to calling the second attorney or to have withdrawn entirely.

C. To have either asked the client's permission prior to calling the second attorney or to have given the associated attorney the greater portion of the fee.

D. To have either asked the client's permission prior to calling the second attorney, to have withdrawn entirely, or to have given the associated attorney the greater portion of the fee.

29. A lawyer accepts an engagement ring from her client in lieu of a $1,000 payment. The ring was worth approximately $1100. Such a fee arrangement is:

A. Improper.

B. Proper.

C. A violation of the Model Rules.

D. None of the above.

30. A client contacts a lawyer to represent him in a criminal case. The client pays the lawyer's fee of $20,000 up front. Despite the lawyer's best efforts in court, the client is

convicted. The client then demands the return of his $20,000. What should the lawyer do?

A. Nothing.

B. Return the fee.

C. Tell the prosecutor.

D. Recommend arbitration of the dispute.

31. A lawyer represents a client in a case involving an alleged contractual misrepresentation the client made to his roommate. At one point, the client says, "If this [expletive] continues, I'm going to have to get someone to kill my roommate."

The lawyer tells the client, "Do not do that. It will only make your problems worse."

The client responds, "Perhaps so, but I'm getting very close to having him taken out, and I mean it."

The lawyer does nothing, and, unfortunately, the roommate is murdered, apparently by the client.

Which of the following is most correct?

A. The lawyer is subject to discipline because he was required to reveal the danger to the roommate.

B. The lawyer is subject to discipline because he was required to withdraw from the case.

C. The lawyer behaved properly because the crime was not reasonably apparent.

D. The lawyer behaved properly because the case involved his client.

32. An attorney is called before the State Bar's disciplinary board regarding the fact that the attorney was told by her client that the client intended to commit tax fraud and the attorney failed to notify the Internal Revenue Service. Which of the following is correct?

A. The attorney is permitted to reveal the conversation between herself and the client to the disciplinary board, because the client had no reasonable expectation that the attorney would keep such information confidential.

B. The attorney is not subject to discipline for failing to notify the Internal Revenue Service. However, the attorney is permitted to reveal the conversation between herself and the client to the disciplinary board, if it is relevant to the attorney's defense.

C. The attorney is subject to discipline.

D. The attorney is subject to discipline only if the Internal Revenue Service has subpoenaed the information from the attorney, because the Internal Revenue Service has the right to know about potential frauds.

33. Questions 33 and 34 relate to the following facts:

Lawyer Lucy is an expert in securities regulation law. Corp, a corporation, retains Lucy's law firm to qualify Corp's stock for public issuance. After accepting the representation, Lucy assigns the matter to Associate Abe, a newly hired associate with Lucy's firm who is just out of law school, so Lucy can pursue other matters. Abe does not want to take the case, telling Lucy that he knows nothing about securities law and doesn't have time to get up to speed on the matter. Lucy tells Abe: "Tough luck. I learned how to sink or swim on my own with these cases and you will, too. I've got no time to hold your hand while you learn how to be a lawyer." Was Lucy's conduct proper in this matter?

A. No, unless Corp had given Lucy express permission to assign an associate to work on the matter.

B. No, because Lucy knew Abe was not competent to handle the matter, and she failed to provide supervision adequate to protect the client's interest.

C. Yes, because as a member of the bar, Abe is licensed to handle any legal matter.

D. Yes, because Lucy could have turned the case down in the first place.

34. Despite his misgivings, Abe agrees to work on the matter. However, as he feared, Abe makes a variety of mistakes that

result in the public offering being invalidated, and Corp being subjected to a variety of lawsuits. A more experienced securities lawyer would not have made such mistakes. Is Abe subject to discipline?

A. Yes, because Abe had a duty to refuse to work on the matter.

B. Yes, because Abe failed to provide competent legal representation.

C. No, as long as he worked diligently on the matter.

D. No, because Abe was entitled to defer to Lucy's judgment that he was competent to handle the matter.

35. Brothers Bobby and Benji are charged with robbery of a gas station and felony murder because the cashier was shot and killed during the robbery. It is alleged that Bobby committed the robbery and killing while Benji waited outside in the car. In fact, the evidence showing that Benji was a knowing participant in the crime is extremely weak. The brothers want Attorney Alpha to represent them jointly, and are willing to waive any conflicts of interest. Alpha expects the D.A. to offer leniency to Benji in exchange for his testimony against Bobby. May Alpha represent both Bobby and Benji concurrently?

A. No, because Alpha cannot reasonably believe that he can represent adequately the interests of both brothers in these circumstances.

B. No, because Federal Rule of Criminal Procedure 44 prohibits joint representation in such circumstances.

C. Yes, unless the brothers' testimony will be directly conflicting.

D. Yes, because the brothers are willing to waive any conflicts of interest.

36. Catina is a longtime client of Tax Attorney Alberto. After filing her most recent tax return, Catina meets with Alberto. She tells Alberto that she took some pretty aggressive positions in preparing the return, and fully expects to get audited by the IRS. She then hands Alberto some paperwork

which contains receipts and calculations relating to the tax return. Catina asks Alberto to hold on to the documents in anticipation of an IRS audit. Alberto agrees and places the paperwork in one of his file cabinets. Is Alberto subject to discipline?

A. Yes, because it is improper for a lawyer to tamper with or conceal evidence.

B. Yes, because a lawyer must turn over the fruits or instrumentalities of a crime that come into the lawyer's possession.

C. No, because what Catina told him about the documents is confidential.

D. No, because there is no duty to turn over evidence of potential wrongdoing before any audit by the IRS.

37. A lawyer agrees to represent a client on a murder case. The client is indigent, so the lawyer agrees to do the case for 50% royalties on a book about the case that the lawyer "may write after the trial is complete." Before the trial, the client pleads guilty to negligent homicide. The lawyer never writes the book and, thus, receives no fee. The lawyer's fee agreement is:

A. Proper, because the client consented.

B. Proper, because there was no actual prejudice.

C. Proper, but only because the book was never written and the case did not go to trial.

D. None of the above.

38. A lawyer worked for one law firm for many years. She then switched to another firm. While at the previous firm, the lawyer had a minor role in a suit against a woman by a client. In the course of that suit, the lawyer learned some confidential information about her then client. While at her new firm, she is approached by a third party regarding representing her in a suit against that former client. The suit is somewhat related to the earlier case. If the attorney accepts the case, she is:

A. Subject to discipline.

B. Subject to discipline, but only if she compromises anything she learned about that former client.

C. Subject to discipline, unless she is screened from any participation in the case.

D. Not subject to discipline.

39. A law firm enters into an agreement to represent a new client. Shortly thereafter, the senior partners learn that one of their new attorneys had represented another individual who was suing that client. Which of the following actions will prevent the partners from being subject to discipline?

A. Immediately terminating the new attorney and then taking the case.

B. Taking the case but screening the new attorney from any participation in the case.

C. Immediately terminating the new attorney, or screening the new attorney from any participation in the case, or obtaining written consent from all involved.

D. Immediately terminating the new attorney or screening the new attorney from any participation in the case.

40. An associate in a small firm once represented a man in a lawsuit against a woman. Sometime later, the associate left and joined a big firm. The woman then contacted the big firm about possible representation. After interviewing her, the firm decided to not take her case. Shortly afterward, one of the big firm's partners left and started his own solo practice. The solo practitioner was then contacted by an individual looking for representation in a lawsuit against the woman. May the solo practitioner take the case?

A. Yes, because there is no longer the imputation of conflict of interest.

B. Yes, because the solo practitioner was never disqualified from this representation.

C. No, because once there has been a conflict of interest, the taint of that conflict can never be vitiated.

D. No.

41. A firm is about to represent a plaintiff who is suing a defendant. However, in the course of their due diligence, they discover that, prior to being hired by the firm, one of their associates once represented someone who had sued the plaintiff. Both opposing counsel and the defendant are made aware of the potential conflict and consent in writing to the firm's representation of the plaintiff, so long as the associate is screened off. Under these facts, are the firm's partners subject to discipline if they take the case?

    A. Yes.

    B. No.

    C. No. However, the associate is subject to discipline if the firm takes the case.

    D. No. However, the associate is subject to discipline because she will probably assist opposing counsel in the case.

42. Lawyer Lacy is admitted to practice law in State A but she is not licensed to practice in State B. Her granddaughter just finished law school and is applying for bar admission in State B. Lawyer Lacy likes her granddaughter well enough but does not trust that she is actually mature enough to handle the practice of law competently. However, she knows that her family would be devastated if her granddaughter did not get her license in State B. Can Lawyer Lacy write a letter stating that her granddaughter is fit to practice law?

    A. No, because Lacy is not a member of the bar of State B.

    B. No, because Lacy would be falsely stating her opinion about her granddaughter's fitness to practice law.

    C. Yes, because it is likely her granddaughter will mature after she begins practice.

    D. Yes, because she is held to a different standard in State A than State B.

43. A lawyer is representing a client accused of theft from a store. The client then asks his lawyer for advice on the best time and way to violently rob a bank, since the lawyer had

spent many years working for banks and would be likely to know the answer. What should the lawyer do?

A. Withdraw from further representation of the client.

B. Inform the managers of the bank that the client intends to rob that bank.

C. Inform the court of the client's intention to violently rob the bank or keep silent; it is up to the lawyer's discretion.

D. Assist the client in the bank robbery so as to minimize injuries to bystanders.

44. A lawyer works for a corporation. The corporation's president is contemplating a complex business transaction that the lawyer believes to be fraudulent. The lawyer informs the president of his belief that the contemplated transaction is fraudulent, but the president says, "I think we'll go ahead anyway." If the lawyer goes directly to the Board of Directors, requesting that they override the president's decision, the lawyer is:

A. Behaving properly.

B. Subject to discipline.

C. Behaving improperly.

D. None of the above.

45. An attorney works as in-house counsel for a corporation. One day, an employee of the corporation approaches the attorney about illegal acts that the employee's direct supervisor has requested the employee to perform, some of which the employee has already performed. What should the attorney do?

A. Tell the corporation that he is no longer the corporation's attorney but will, instead, be the employee's attorney from here on out.

B. Counsel against the fraud.

C. Tell the employee that the attorney is not the employee's lawyer.

D. Tell the employee not to be concerned about his past fraudulent actions.

46. Plaintiff Polly slips, falls, and injures herself while shopping in a Whole Grains supermarket. Polly sues Whole Grains in Federal Court and alleges that the store negligently caused her injury by placing too much wax on its floor, making it unreasonably slippery. In response to the lawsuit, Whole Grains' CEO hires Lawyer Lucas to conduct an investigation to determine the merits of Polly's claim. During the course of his investigation, Lucas interviews Janitor Jones, who is responsible for waxing the floors in the supermarket. During discovery, Polly's Attorney Abe makes a discovery request for "the results of any internal investigation relating to the claim." Is Abe entitled to the results from Lucas' interview with Jones?

   A. No, pursuant to the corporate attorney-client privilege from *Upjohn v. United States*.

   B. No, because each side must do its own work in preparing a lawsuit for trial.

   C. Yes, because Jones is not part of Whole Grains' control group and is not of manager status.

   D. Yes, as long as Jones consents.

47. A lawyer agrees to represent a criminal defendant. Since the defendant is hard pressed for cash, the lawyer agrees to accept an expensive watch as an advance on the first $10,000 owed. Since the lawyer has not earned the $10,000 yet, he is in a quandary as to what to do with the watch. What is the lawyer's best course of conduct?

   A. Wear the watch.

   B. Sell the watch and put the $10,000 in his client trust account.

   C. Place the watch in a client-only safety deposit box.

   D. Give the watch to his girlfriend.

48. Attorney Alex represented Husband Hugh and Wife Winona in setting up their family business, a restaurant. During the course of the representation, Alex became highly familiar

with the personal financial circumstances of both Hugh and Winona. Running the business puts a strain on the couple's marriage, and Hugh and Winona decide to divorce. Winona is served with a divorce petition from Hugh. After reading the petition, Winona notices that Alex is representing Hugh in the divorce case. Angry, Winona calls Hugh to complain. A short time later, Winona receives a letter from Alex asking her to consent in writing to his representation of Hugh in the divorce. Winona reluctantly agrees. Has Alex acted properly?

A. Yes, because there is no substantial relationship between the divorce case and the business representation.

B. Yes, because he obtained a conflict waiver from Winona.

C. No, because the conflict in the divorce case was not waivable.

D. No, because Winona's conflict waiver came after the representation had already begun.

49. Insured Ivan is involved in a car accident. Pursuant to the terms of his insurance contract, his insurance company, Insco, provides Ivan with Attorney Alison to represent him in the ensuing litigation. There is no separate retainer agreement governing the representation. During the course of the representation, Ivan admits to Alison that he had been drinking prior to the accident. Alison includes this information in the monthly summary she prepares for Insco regarding each of the cases she handles on behalf of the company. As a result, Insco writes a letter to Ivan informing him that his policy does not cover accidents involving the use of alcohol. Has Alison acted properly?

A. No, because Ivan's confession was confidential.

B. No, because Ivan was the primary client and Insco the secondary client.

C. Yes, because she could not assist Ivan in defrauding Insco.

D. Yes, because Ivan committed a crime by drinking and driving.

50. A lawyer settles a case on behalf of a client for a significant amount of money. The lawyer, unknown to the client, then invests the entire settlement in a business gamble and wins big. He then confesses this to the client and offers the client half of his profits in addition to the amount of money that the client owed as part of the settlement. Is the lawyer subject to discipline?

    A. Yes, because he has commingled funds.

    B. Yes, because lawyers must not gamble.

    C. No, because there was no harm to the client.

    D. No, because the client profited substantially.

51. A lawyer wins a lot of money on behalf of a client. The lawyer promptly distributes the client's money to the client. However, the lawyer keeps his own fees in the client trust account for two more months, so as to avoid paying taxes. If the lawyer is called before the State Bar for discipline, the State Bar's best argument in favor of disciplining the lawyer is:

    A. There was harm to the client.

    B. There was commingling.

    C. Lawyers are never allowed to try to minimize their taxes.

    D. The lawyer should have closed the client trust account immediately upon the conclusion of this case.

52. A lawyer is representing a client on a "slip and fall" case. The lawyer is performing excellent work and is nearing settlement of the case. For no good reason, the client terminates the lawyer's employment. Under these circumstances, the lawyer:

    A. Should withdraw.

    B. Shall withdraw.

    C. May withdraw.

    D. Should seek arbitration.

53. An attorney is an excellent and tough lawyer. She is representing a client in a civil rights action. In order to motivate the opposing party to settle, she attempts to "wear down" his desire to sue. She does this by opposing every discovery request and by making several discovery requests that are not necessary. Is the attorney subject to discipline?

    A. No, because this is an acceptable tactic.

    B. No, because ours is an adversary system.

    C. No, because discovery is, per se, acceptable.

    D. Yes.

54. State X and State Y each have state trademark registration statutes that are substantially similar in purpose and wording to the Lanham Act (the federal trademark registration statute). For many years, Daisy Dairy has used the mark "Daisy" on dairy projects it sells in State X, and it has registered the mark under the State X statute. Recently Noxatox Chemical began using the "Daisy" mark on cockroach poison it sells in State X. Daisy Dairy sued Noxatox under State X law in a State X court for intentional infringement of the "Daisy" mark. The complaint asked for an injunction, an award of the profits made by Noxatox, and money damages. Noxatox moved for summary judgment on the grounds that dairy products and cockroach poison do not compete with each other, that no sensible consumer could be deceived by the use of the same mark on such widely different goods, and that Daisy Dairy could not possibly have suffered monetary injury. The trial judge who will hear the motion is not well versed in trademark law, and the lawyer for Daisy Dairy failed to discover several pertinent court decisions. Which of the following decisions MUST the lawyer for Noxatox call to the judge's attention?

    I. A United States Supreme Court decision which holds that the Lanham Act authorizes an injunction to stop intentional infringement, even where the defendant's goods do not compete with the plaintiff's goods.

    II. A decision of the United States Court of Appeals for the circuit that includes State X and State Y, holding that an injunction can be issued under the Lanham Act where the nature of the defendant's goods could cast a distasteful or odious image on the plaintiff's goods.

III. A decision of the Supreme Court of State Y which holds that the State Y registration statute authorizes an accounting of the defendant's profits in a case of intentional infringement, even where the plaintiff cannot prove monetary injury.

IV. A decision of the Supreme Court of State X which holds that in actions for intentional trespass to real property, State X trial judges have the power of courts of equity to fashion equitable remedies, even where the plaintiff cannot prove monetary injury.

A. All of the above.

B. None of the above.

C. I, II, and IV only.

D. I and IV only.

55. A lawyer is representing a client in a complex securities case. The opposing counsel has failed to cite two cases on two different points. Both are directly on point. One case is in State P (where this case is being litigated.) The other case is in sister State Q (State P usually follows the lead of State Q.) The lawyer reveals neither case to the court. Moreover, in closing argument, the lawyer alludes to facts that she did not offer in the case-in-chief (she believes she can "get this by" the inattentive and ill-informed jury.) The opposing party prevails in the verdict. Which of the following will subject the lawyer to discipline?

A. Losing the case.

B. Not revealing the State P case, as well as the lawyer's closing argument.

C. Not revealing the State Q case.

D. The lawyer's failure to inform opposing counsel about the opposing cases outside of court.

56. A client tells his attorney that he must perjure himself regarding the use of self-defense. The attorney tries to

convince the client not to proceed, but the client is adamant. The attorney makes a decision that it is better that she help. She coaches the client on the best way to use this defense. Utilizing the perjury, the client is acquitted.

A. The attorney is subject to discipline, but is not subject to malpractice liability.

B. The attorney is not subject to discipline, but is subject to malpractice liability.

C. The attorney is subject to discipline and is also subject to malpractice liability.

D. The attorney is neither subject to discipline nor to malpractice liability.

57. Client Fujitomi entrusted Lawyer Lee with $10,000, to be used six weeks later to close a business transaction. Lee immediately deposited it in her client trust account; at the time, it was the only money in that account. Later that same day, the local bar association called Lee and asked her to rush out to the Municipal Court to take over the defense of an indigent drunkard, Watkins, who was being tried for violating an obscure municipal statute. Because of chaos in the Public Defender's Office, Watkins was being tried without benefit of counsel. By the time Lee arrived, the judge had already found Watkins guilty and sentenced him to pay a fine of $350 or spend 30 days in jail. Under a peculiar local rule of court, the only way to keep Watkins from going to jail was to pay the fine immediately and to request a trial de novo in the Superior Court. Therefore, Lee paid the fine with a check drawn on her client trust account, and Watkins promised to repay her within one week. Which one of the following statements is correct?

A. Lee's handling of the Watkins matter was proper.

B. Lee would have been subject to litigation sanction if she had allowed Watkins to go to jail.

C. If Lee had paid Watkins' fine out of her personal bank account, that action would have been proper.

D. Lee would be subject to discipline for handling the matter in any manner other than she did.

58. An attorney holds a pretrial news conference regarding his client's case. The client was allegedly beaten up by the police without provocation. The attorney's motivation for holding the news conference is to motivate the other side to settle. On these facts alone, the attorney's conduct is:

    A. Proper.

    B. Not proper.

    C. In violation of the disciplinary rules.

    D. Not proper because the attorney's motivation is in violation of the disciplinary rules.

59. At the close of a lawyer's case, after a verdict has been obtained in favor of the lawyer's client, the lawyer takes the stand to state her fees (which the losing party must pay). This action is:

    A. Proper.

    B. Not proper.

    C. In violation of the disciplinary rules.

    D. Not proper, because disclosure of the lawyer's fee is in violation of the attorney-client privilege.

60. A lawyer is representing a man in a case against a woman. The woman is being represented by an attorney from a nearby city. The man's lawyer calls the woman's attorney repeatedly to make an objectively fair offer of settlement. The attorney does not return the lawyer's calls. The man's lawyer then makes a written settlement offer with the request that, even if the offer is rejected, the woman's attorney must make phone or written contact. Still, the woman's attorney makes no contact. Finally, the man's lawyer contacts the woman directly. The woman is shocked that such generous offers were made and that the woman had never heard about them. The woman's attorney files a complaint with the State Bar against the man's lawyer for "interfering in the sacrosanct attorney-client relationship." This complaint will:

    A. Fail, because of the bad faith of the woman's attorney.

B. Fail, because the man's lawyer had no reasonable alternative.

C. Fail, because no settlement was actually made.

D. None of the above.

End of MPRE Simulated Exam 1.

Sample MPRE Exam 1 Answer Explanations

1. A is the correct answer. Lucy may properly grant the delay of one week. The issue in this question concerns Rule 1.2, Scope of Representation. Under Rule 1.2, the client directs the objectives of the representation but the lawyer is permitted to direct the means or strategies to achieve those objectives. Here, Paula wanted Lucy to "observe every technicality." Technically, Lucy could have objected to the delay. However, the details of the representation are properly left to the lawyer and a court would have likely granted Donald an extension under these circumstances. Lucy, as the lawyer, is permitted to make this call.

   B is incorrect because "fault" as to why the delay occurred does not come into play in this analysis.

   C is incorrect because although Lucy certainly owes her client a duty of loyalty, the duty of loyalty is not breached here by permitting the short delay.

   D is incorrect because Lucy does not need Paula to agree to the extension.

2. D is the correct answer. Here, Alfred has a valid legal basis for requesting that the Council redo the vote. Under Rule 3.1, Meritorious Claims and Contentions, Alfred would only be violating this rule if the lawsuit were frivolous. However, nothing prevents Alfred from bringing a technically valid lawsuit requesting the Council to comply with the law. The fact that the delay caused by the lawsuit is more beneficial to Alfred's client than the actual result of the lawsuit does not change the analysis.

   A is incorrect because nothing in the facts suggests that the difference between a voice ballot and a secret ballot is frivolous.

B is incorrect because "delay" can be a wise strategy for Alfred's client and this alone is not problematic unless there is no basis in law or fact for the lawsuit.

C is incorrect because we are not required to assess under the rules whether there is a proper purpose or not. The standard is whether the lawsuit is frivolous.

3. C is the correct answer. This type of question is called an Option Type of Question and they are typically challenging. You can handle these best through a process of eliminating a wrong answer option, and then eliminating answer choices with that option. Here, Option I. is correct. Under Rule 3.6, Trial Publicity, an attorney can provide limited information to the public in terms of trial publicity as long as it does not prejudice the case. Option I is permissible because it states what is in the public record, i.e., the pleadings. Option II is not permissible nor is it relevant. It would be considered an extrajudicial statement that could prejudice the proceedings, and therefore, this would be disallowed under Rule 3.6. Option III is correct because a lawyer is allowed to request the public's help in identifying key witnesses or individuals with needed information. Therefore, Answer choice C is correct because it properly states the correct options of I and III, but not II.

   A is incorrect because the question allows only one answer Option, i.e., either II only or III only.

   B is incorrect because the question allows only one answer Option, i.e., either II only or III only.

   D is incorrect because it contains Option II which is not permissible.

4. D is the correct answer. Under Rule 1.5, it is improper to charge an excessive or unreasonable fee. Under Rule 8.3, Reporting Professional Misconduct, an attorney who "knows that another lawyer has committed a violation of the Rules of Professional Conduct that raises a substantial question as to that lawyer's honesty, trustworthiness or fitness as a lawyer in other respects, shall inform the appropriate professional authority." Here, Lois knows Albert violated the rules, i.e., violated Rule 1.5, and this was clearly

dishonest as Albert himself admits that that he lied in his statement. Therefore, under Rule 8.3, Lois is required to report Albert.

A is incorrect because the client's opinion does nothing to change the duty Lois has under Rule 8.3.

B is incorrect because under the rules, there is no assessment of "damage" to a client; in other words, a client does not have to be damaged in order for there to be a violation of the rules (a damage assessment, however, *is required* for malpractice). Here, Albert clearly violated Rule 1.5 and that is sufficient.

C is incorrect because whether Lois believes it was a mistake or not is irrelevant.

5. D is the correct answer. Under Rule 7.1, advertisements must not be misleading. A statement that a lawyer has never lost a case, even if true, is misleading because it sets up an unreasonable expectation regarding cases that no lawyer could claim. Quinn's ad is in violation of the rules.

   A is incorrect because lawyer advertising is given limited First Amendment protection.

   B is incorrect because lawyer advertising has limited First Amendment protection.

   C is incorrect because there is no requirement that lawyer ads appear in a dignified forum.

6. C is the correct answer. Lawyers must not lie on their bar applications. To knowingly make a false statement of material fact shows a lack of good character, which subjects an attorney to discipline (Rule 8.1). Here, the woman lied on her bar application by concealing her suspension for marijuana use while she was in college. Thus, she is subject to discipline.

   A is incorrect because discipline is not for the purpose of punishment. Rather, it is to protect the public from dangerously inept or corrupt attorneys. Moreover, there are no statutes of limitations regarding disciplining attorneys.

B is incorrect because it is permissible to discipline an attorney for past acts unrelated to her present psychological state.

D is incorrect because discipline is not for the purpose of punishment. Rather, it is to protect the public from dangerously inept or corrupt attorneys.

7. C is the correct answer. A lawyer must turn in his delinquent peers provided that what they know is unprivileged (Rule 8.3(a)). Here, the boss is not the lawyer's client. Thus, the lawyer's knowledge of the boss's embezzling of funds is not privileged information.

   A is incorrect, since the silence is not proper for the reasons discussed in C, and even the attorney's request for the boss to turn himself in (Answer B) does not relieve the attorney of the duty to turn in a delinquent peer (the boss).

   B is incorrect for the reasons above, i.e., that the attorney's request for the boss to turn himself in does not relieve the attorney of the duty to turn in a delinquent peer.

   D is incorrect for two reasons. First, the lawyer's silence is not in good faith (since the attorney knows that the boss's activities are improper). Second, good faith is not an excuse for this kind of violation. (Note: California has no such requirement. However, the California rules are not tested on the MPRE. They *are* tested in the essay portion of the California Bar Examination.)

8. D is the correct answer. A state can discipline a lawyer for actions performed anywhere if such actions involve moral turpitude. Since manslaughter is morally wrong, discipline is acceptable, even if it occurred in another State (Rules 8.4 and 8.5).

   A is incorrect for the reasons discussed in Answer D.

   B is incorrect because moral turpitude does not need to be related to the practice of law.

   C is incorrect because the actions of moral turpitude need not be directly related to the practice of law.

9. A is the correct answer. Judges should not be character witnesses because it appears improper. Code of Judicial Conduct, Rule 3.3. Here, the man has asked his friend who is a municipal judge to be a character witness. It would be improper for the judge to be one.

   B is incorrect because judges may on occasion be required to testify, e.g., if they are a party to their own litigation.

   C is incorrect because the man's good or bad character is not the issue. The issue is whether the judge is permitted to testify.

   D is incorrect because a judge should not be a character witness.

10. C is the correct answer choice. Again, this is an Options Question so the best course of action is to go through each option to determine which ones are correct and incorrect. Option I is a correct option. Under Rule 1.15, Client Trust Accounts, an attorney cannot commingle client funds with attorney funds. Further, any amount in dispute needs to be kept in the Client Trust Account. Here, Lawyer billed client for $5000. Client agreed that Lawyer earned $3000 but there was $2000 in dispute. Lawyer has a couple of different options as to how to handle this, but the main concern is not to commingle funds. Option I is correct because Lawyer should send the client the $20,000 that is client's award. Lawyer can keep the $5000 in the Client Trust Account because that amount of Lawyer's fee is in dispute. Option II is also correct. Here, Lawyer can send the $20,000 to client. Lawyer is required to keep any disputed amount in the Client Trust Account. Here, $2000 is in dispute; $3000 is not in dispute. Lawyer can properly transfer the amount "earned" and not in dispute to lawyer's office account. (As in Option I, Lawyer could have left the whole $5000 in the Client Trust Account as well). Option II, however, is not correct. Because there is $2000 in dispute, Lawyer cannot put the full amount into his office account.

    A is incorrect because it does not contain the correct options.

    B is incorrect because it does not contain the correct options.

D is incorrect because it does not contain the correct options.

11. C is the correct answer. Under Code of Judicial Conduct, Rule 3.15(A)(1), a judge is permitted to teach law and be paid. Judges should also make a public report of their extra judicial income.

    A is incorrect because a judge would be allowed to teach law.

    B is incorrect for the same reason.

    D is incorrect for the same reason.

12. C is the correct answer. Judges are permitted to manage and participate in the investment of their financial resources. A judge must avoid financial and business dealings that would reasonably appear to exploit the judge's judicial position. Code of Judicial Conduct, Rule 3.11(A).

    A is incorrect because a judge may manage or participate in investments whether or not the judge does well.

    B is incorrect because judges cannot do anything they want. Their conduct is controlled by the Code of Judicial Conduct.

    D is incorrect because the business can be related to law, e.g., law teaching. Code of Judicial Conduct, Rule 3.1, Comment [1].

13. D is the correct answer. Under Rule 1.5, a lawyer's fee must be reasonable. Here, Lucy's fees were significantly more than other lawyers in the jurisdiction and were unreasonable.

    A is wrong because whether the client wins or not is irrelevant to a discipline issue.

    B is incorrect because although $200 per hour is reasonable for an hourly fee, Lucy's overall fees were unreasonable.

    C is incorrect because even if Lucy did work all of the hours, the fee would still be unreasonable.

14. A is the correct answer. Judges, when campaigning for office, generally should not make pledges regarding the way they would sentence. Code of Judicial Conduct, Rule 4.3, Comment [1]. However, in this case, the lawyer/candidate is simply stating that the candidate will order the maximum

sentence. This is not a specific comment about any particular case or particular area of law, and therefore, this is permissible. The First Amendment does allow a judicial candidates to make general statements about what he/she intends to do if elected.

B is incorrect because the First Amendment is applicable to judges, so judges can take a "law and order" stance.

C is incorrect because ample facts were given.

D is incorrect because the First Amendment controls in all United States jurisdictions.

15. C is the correct answer. Passing the bar exam, on its face, is proof of reasonable competence. Perhaps where the law is complex, a new lawyer should not begin practice in that area. But in any general area of law, new lawyers are permitted to start right out (Rule 1.1). Here, criminal law is a general area of law in which anyone who has passed the bar exam is presumed competent.

    A is incorrect for the same reason that C is correct.

    B is incorrect because no facts indicate that the lawyer is actually incompetent.

    D is incorrect because no facts indicate that the lawyer is actually competent.

16. A is the correct answer. Under Rule 1.7, a lawyer cannot represent concurrent clients with interests adverse to each other unless the attorney believes she can do so and the client gives informed, written consent. Here, although it may initially seem like the clients would be adverse to each other, even a conflict with a current client can be overcome with client's written, informed consent. (Note that it would be rare for a client to actually do this but the rules do permit it and that is what the MPRE tests). A correctly states the requirement that to get around a concurrent conflict of interest, you can obtain a client's written, informed consent.

    B is incorrect because there is nothing in the conflicts rules that require a waiver of confidentiality.

C is incorrect because under Rule 1.7, a lawyer can get around a conflict through informed, written consent.

D is incorrect because although a lawyer does owe the client a duty of loyalty, this does not trump the ability for a client to waive a conflict under Rule 1.7.

17. A is the correct answer. As a general rule, strategy is entirely within a lawyer's discretion. There are, however, certain fundamental choices that are entirely to be made by the client. Whether or not to take the stand is one of those areas (Rule 1.2(a)). Thus, the lawyer should have let the client testify.

    B is incorrect because if a client disagrees as to strategy, the lawyer may follow his own decisions and desires.

    C is incorrect because the real issue is not what the jury might think but rather, the client's right to take the stand.

    D is incorrect for the same reasons that A is correct.

18. C is the correct answer. A lawyer must not make use of perjured testimony (Rules 3.3(a)(3) and 3.3(b)). The lawyer not only plans to make use of the client's perjured testimony, he also aids in the fraud on the court by coaching the client as to how to lie on the stand.

    A is incorrect for the same reasons that C is correct.

    B is incorrect because a technical violation of the mandatory rules subjects an attorney to discipline. Of course, if it is merely a technical violation, the discipline would probably be light, e.g., a private reprimand only.

    D is incorrect for the same reasons that C is correct.

19. C is the correct answer. There is nothing in the code that prohibits a lawyer from charging low fees. On the contrary, lawyers are encouraged to compete and also to do some pro bono work (work for free) (Rule 6.1). Thus, the lawyer's undercutting of fees is within his own discretion and is, thus, "proper."

    Choices A, B and D are incorrect for the same reasons that C is correct.

20. B is the correct answer because there is an exception to the rule barring solicitation of clients when the solicitation concerns a former client (Rule 7.3(a)(2)). When a client is to be prejudiced, as is the case here (because the will needs to be changed, since the sole beneficiary is now deceased), the best course of conduct is for the attorney to initiate contact with that former client (on the related matter). Rule 1.3.

    A is incorrect for the reasons discussed in B.

    C is incorrect because, although lawyers "should" contact clients in like situations, such contact is within their discretion, unless of course, they tell the client that they will periodically inspect the legal document. Because this is a matter for attorney discretion, not doing so will not subject the attorney to discipline.

    D is incorrect for the reasons discussed in B.

21. B is the correct answer. For the most part, attorneys can set their own fees, which are permitted to be substantial within the broad parameters of reasonableness. Rule 1.5.

    A is incorrect because, although excessive fees will subject an attorney to discipline, this fee was likely not excessive, for the reasons discussed in B.

    C is incorrect because attorney fees must be reasonable.

    D is incorrect because, although excessive fees will subject an attorney to discipline, this fee was likely not excessive, for the reasons discussed in B.

22. C is the correct answer. Expertise is a factor in determining whether the attorney fee is excessive or reasonable. The attorney's fame (reputation) is another legitimate factor. The more difficult the case, the higher the fee can be. Although not completely controlling, the fees of similarly situated attorneys are relevant in determining whether a particular attorney's fee is excessive. See generally Rule 1.5.

    A is incorrect because it does not include all of these factors.

    B is incorrect because it does not include all of these factors.

D is incorrect because the fees charged by one particular competitor are not taken into account in determining the reasonableness of an attorney's fees.

23. B is the correct answer. Rule 3.3, Candor to the Tribunal, requires a lawyer to correct any false testimony made by a client. Here, however, Patty answered the question truthfully. B is correct in that Patty's testimony was "literally" true. The attorney for the employer did not ask about other narcotics, and Lucas is under no obligation to offer additional information (which would actually breach Lucas' duty of confidentiality to Patty).

    A is incorrect because although an attorney does owe a duty of confidentiality to all clients, this is not the rule applicable to this question.

    C is incorrect because Lucas can comply with the duty of candor to the court since Patty was technically truthful.

    D is incorrect because this misstates the rule; an attorney has no duty under Rule 3.3 to correct "inferences."

24. A is the correct answer. Nothing in the Code requires an attorney to accept all walk-in clients. The fees need only be reasonable. Rule 1.5. Attorneys are encouraged to perform some legal work for the poor for no charge, but are not required to do so. Rule 6.1.

    B is incorrect because a client is free to contact law firms of any size and attempt to negotiate a fee.

    C is incorrect because the fee must only be reasonable.

    D is incorrect because a client can negotiate a fee.

25. D is the correct answer. Allowing the client to pay an additional $1,500 only if he is acquitted is essentially a contingency fee contract. Contingency fee contracts in criminal cases are per se prohibited. Rule 1.5(d)(2).

    A is incorrect because the attorney's good faith is no defense.

    B is incorrect because the attorney's good faith is no defense.

    C is incorrect because the *Leon* case is not relevant here. In the *Leon* case, the Connecticut attorney charged a fee that he did not earn, and he failed to properly communicate with the client or even prosecute the client's case. Here, the client lost his case, but there is nothing in the facts to indicate that this was due to the attorney's failure to communicate with the client or adequately prosecute the case. Thus, the *Leon* case is irrelevant here. (Note: California law does not, per se, prohibit such an arrangement. However, the MPRE does not test the California rules.)

26. A is the correct answer, because attorney fees need only be reasonable, not equal. Rule 1.5.

    B is incorrect for the same reasons that A is correct.

    C is incorrect because the fees must only be reasonable. Furthermore, there is no State action; thus, the Equal Protection Clause is not relevant.

    D is incorrect because a court only assesses the reasonableness of the fees.

27. D is the correct answer. Fee splits with attorneys outside the firm are acceptable if the client consents and the fee is not raised. Rule 1.5(e) and Rule 1.5 Comment [7]. Here, the client agreed and the fee was not raised. Thus, the attorney is not subject to discipline under these facts.

    A is incorrect because a lawyer can split fees under certain circumstances.

    B is incorrect because it misstates the facts. This fee split was in proportion to actual attorney work performed.

    C is incorrect because the client did consent to this fee split.

28. A is the correct answer because the original attorney must have asked his client's permission prior to even contacting the second attorney. Rule 1.5(e).

    B is incorrect because withdrawal is not necessary.

    C is incorrect because the code does not suggest that disproportionate attorney fee splits are always preferable.

    D is incorrect because an attorney does not have to withdraw.

29. B is the correct answer. Although the receipt of client chattels as payment of the fee is not preferable, it is not

prohibited. See Rule 1.5, Comment [4]. Here, the engagement ring is a client chattel. Thus, the attorney does not violate any of the Model Rules in accepting it.

A is incorrect because it is not prohibited to accept an item in lieu of a fee.

C is incorrect because an engagement ring can suffice as a fee.

D is incorrect because an engagement ring can suffice as a fee.

30. D is the correct answer. When there is a fee dispute between the lawyer and client, the lawyer should recommend arbitration. However, it is not required. See Rule 1.5, Comment [9]. (Note: it would be a different fact pattern entirely if the funds were in the attorney's trust account. This is not the case when the fee is paid up front, as here.)

    A is incorrect for the same reason that D is correct, i.e., that arbitration is recommended.

    B is incorrect because lawyers are not required to return fees that they reasonably believe they have earned.

    C is incorrect because lawyers must not threaten or harm clients so as to keep fees that are in dispute. Telling the prosecutor might appear to be a threat.

31. D is the correct answer. Somewhat surprisingly, there is no requirement that an attorney reveal an intended future crime of her client. The option is given if the crime involves physical danger or corporate fraud under Rule 1.6. Here, although the crime involved physical danger, the lawyer had the option, but not the requirement, to warn the victim. The lawyer in this case chose to honor the attorney-client privilege instead.

    A is incorrect for the same reason that D is correct.

    B is incorrect because an attorney need only withdraw when the crime (or fraud) is on the court itself.

    C is incorrect because it misreads the facts—the crime was reasonably apparent.

32. B is the correct answer. An attorney is permitted to keep to herself her client's spoken intent to commit a future fraud. Rule 1.6(b)(2). Furthermore, an attorney is permitted to reveal a confidence if it is reasonably related to and reasonably necessary to defending herself. Rule 1.6(b)(5).

    A is incorrect because it is irrelevant whether the client had a reasonable expectation that the information would be kept in confidence. Except where permitted by the rules, attorneys must keep all client conversations confidential regardless of the client's apparent reasonable expectations.

    C is incorrect because an attorney does not have to reveal a client's confidence.

    D is incorrect because an attorney does not have to reveal a client's confidence in all circumstances.

33. B is the correct answer. Under Rule 5.1, an attorney is required to supervise other attorneys when the more experienced attorney gives work. Here, Lucy knew that Abe was a new lawyer who was inexperienced in securities work. Her statement that she had had to learn by "sinking" or "swimming" is irrelevant; she had a duty under Rule 5.1 to supervise Abe and she will be responsible for Abe's negligence.

    A is incorrect because the law firm did not have to approve Abe working on the case.

    C is incorrect because although Abe is presumed to be competent as a licensed attorney, this does not mean that Abe can handle "any legal matter." Clearly, the rule of competence contemplates that lawyers need to study and associate with more experienced attorneys when they are taking on a new matter.

    D is incorrect because an attorney is required to supervise other attorneys.

34. B is the correct answer. Under Rule 1.1, a lawyer must provide competent service. Here, if Abe was unsure of how to handle the securities issue, he was obligated to "gain competence" by either studying the area and/or associating with another lawyer with experience in that area. Just

because Lucy was not willing to help him did not take away Abe's obligation to render competent legal work. Abe was required under Rule 1.1 to gain competence, i.e., ask another lawyer.

A is incorrect because there is no duty to refuse work; in fact, the rules allow new lawyers to take on work, but to do so in a competent manner.

C is incorrect because Abe is required to be competent as well as diligent.

D is incorrect because Abe had his own ethical obligations; these are not negated simply because Lucy was his supervising attorney.

35. A is correct. Under Rule 1.7, a lawyer cannot undertake representation of clients that have interests adverse to each other. This conflict can be waived in some circumstances if the lawyer reasonably believes he can represent both parties, and the clients give informed, written consent. However, there are certain nonwaivable (sometimes called non-consentable) conflicts. Two examples are joint clients in a criminal cases and parties in a domestic relations (divorce) case. Here, there is clearly a conflict; further, the conflict is not waivable by the clients.

    B is incorrect because Rule 1.7 disallows the representation, not Rule 44 of the Rules of Criminal Procedure.

    C is incorrect because although true, i.e., the brothers will have conflicting testimony, this is not the reason why the representation is inappropriate.

    D is incorrect because the conflict cannot be waived.

36. D is the correct answer. Under Rule 3.4, Fairness to the Parties, a party is not allowed to obstruct another party's access to evidence. Here, Alberto is not obstructing access to evidence; there is no case against the client yet and he is under no obligation to turn over evidence for a potential case.

    A is incorrect because although a lawyer cannot tamper with evidence, the facts do not suggest that Alberto was tampering with evidence.

B is incorrect because there is no crime yet, if at all.

C is incorrect because although confidentiality always applies, that is not the issue here. And the duty of confidentiality would not allow Alberto, if there was a case by the IRS, to conceal or obstruct evidence.

37. D is the correct answer. An attorney is not permitted to receive as his fee rights to a book about the subject matter of the litigation. Rule 1.8(d).

    A is incorrect because an attorney cannot retain literary rights.

    B is incorrect because an attorney cannot retain literary rights.

    C is incorrect because an attorney cannot retain literary rights. (Note: California law may permit such an arrangement. See California Business and Professions Code §§ 6146–6149.5 and California Rules of Professional Conduct, Rule 4–200. However, the California rules, while tested on the California Bar Examination, are not tested on the MPRE.)

38. A is the correct answer. When a lawyer has learned something confidential and relevant about a client, she is not permitted to oppose that client in a later case. Rule 1.9(a).

    B is incorrect because it misreads the facts. The facts indicate that the prior confidence is "somewhat related." Thus, the lawyer cannot take the case.

    C is incorrect because screening the lawyer from participation in the case is not an option under the facts, which indicate that she accepts the case.

    D is incorrect for the same reason that A is correct.

39. C is the correct answer. When a lawyer in a firm is disqualified, generally all lawyers in the firm are disqualified. Rule 1.10. Here, the firm would be disqualified because of the direct conflict of interest caused by the fact that the new attorney had previously represented a party adverse to the new client. Although terminating the new

attorney is harsh and may open the firm to civil liability for wrongful termination, the termination will remove the conflict of interest. Screening the attorney from participation in the case is acceptable, provided there is written consent from all involved.

A is incorrect because of the imputation of conflict rules.

B is incorrect because of the imputation of conflict rules.

D is incorrect because of the imputation of conflict rules.

40. A is the correct answer. A vicariously disqualified attorney (here the solo practitioner) is no longer disqualified if he discontinues an association with the disqualified attorney (the associate). See generally Rule 1.10. In this case, the big firm was disqualified from representing the woman because the associate had once represented a party adverse to the woman. This disqualification was imputed to everyone else at the firm. However, once the solo practitioner left and started his own solo practice, he was no longer vicariously disqualified.

    B is incorrect because, as discussed above, the solo practitioner was vicariously disqualified only while working at the big firm. However, once he left and started his own solo practice, he was no longer disqualified.

    C is incorrect because the imputation rules under Rule 1.10 apply.

    D is incorrect because of the imputation rules of Rule 1.10.

41. B is the correct answer. Disqualification can be waived by the opposing party. Thus, since such a waiver occurred here, B is the correct answer. Rule 1.10(c).

    A is incorrect because in no way does it appear that the firm's lawyers compromised his case. The associate had to be screened from participation in the case.

    C is incorrect because, as discussed above, disqualification can be waived by the opposing party, as it has been here. Thus, neither the firm nor the associate will be subject to discipline under these facts.

D is incorrect since no facts whatsoever suggest that the associate will assist opposing counsel.

42. B is the correct answer. If Lacy tells the bar of State B that her granddaughter is fit to practice law when she believes the opposite, then Lacy is knowingly making a false statement of fact in violation of Rule 8.1(a).

    A is incorrect because State A can discipline Lacy for actions that she took in State B. Rule 8.5 allows a lawyer to be disciplined even when the activity occurs in a different state.

    C is incorrect because the issue is whether Lacy made a dishonest statement of fact. State A can discipline her regardless of where the conduct occurred.

    D is incorrect because the issue is whether Lacy was dishonest. If Lacy made a dishonest statement then she can be disciplined by State A even if the conduct occurred in State B.

43. C is the correct answer. A lawyer may reveal to a court a client's intentions to commit a crime involving potential serious bodily harm or death. Rule 1.6(b)(1). Here, violently robbing a bank is an action that involves potential serious bodily harm. Thus, the lawyer may reveal to the court the client's intention to commit this action. Note that the rule says that the lawyer may reveal this. It does not say that the lawyer must reveal it. Hence, it is within the lawyer's discretion whether or not to reveal the actions here. (Note that under California Business and Professions Code § 6068(e)(2), California lawyers are given similar discretion. The California rules are not tested on the MPRE, but they are tested in the essay portion of the California Bar Examination.)

    A is incorrect because the lawyer is not required to withdraw; he is merely given the discretion to inform the court if he so chooses, as discussed in C.

    B is incorrect because informing the bank managers would be a violation of the attorney-client privilege; the rules allow the lawyer to inform the court, not the managers of a private business (such as a bank).

D is incorrect because there is no rule that permits lawyers to commit crimes; in fact, they are subject to discipline, as well as criminal liability, for doing so.

44. A is the correct answer. Going over the head of the individual in the business entity who intends to do the fraud is the correct course of conduct. Thus, A is correct. Rule 1.13(b). Here, the lawyer intends to tell the Board of Directors about the president's proposed fraudulent transaction. He is therefore complying with the rule.

B is incorrect because under Rule 1.13, a lawyer can go up the chain of command to disclose in order to prevent harm to the corporate client.

C. is incorrect because under Rule 1.13, a lawyer can go up the chain of command to disclose in order to prevent harm to the corporate client.

D is incorrect because under Rule 1.13, a lawyer can go up the chain of command to disclose to prevent harm to the corporate client.

45. C is the correct answer. The attorney is in a difficult position. Not only should he counsel the direct supervisor and the corporation, but he also may have some duties to the employee who apparently is seeking the attorney's legal advice. What the employee says may hurt the employee if revealed, but may possibly aid the corporation. Therefore, the attorney should, as soon as possible, tell the employee that he represents the corporation, not the employee. Otherwise, there might arise an impermissible conflict of interest between the duties owed to the corporation and those owed to the employee. Without this kind of warning, the employee's interests might be severely compromised. See Rule 1.13, Comment [10].

A is incorrect because the attorney, over the course of his employment with the corporation, has already learned many corporate secrets. Even if the attorney withdraws from representing the corporation, the attorney's duties to safeguard these secrets will remain. However, in representing the employee, the attorney may have to reveal these secrets. Thus, because there is a potential conflict, the attorney should not represent the employee, even if he withdraws from representation of the corporation.

B is incorrect because counseling against the fraud constitutes legal advice, as does telling the employee not to worry about his past fraudulent conduct. As discussed in C, the attorney is not the employee's lawyer. Thus, he should not be giving legal advice to the employee.

D is incorrect because counseling against the fraud constitutes legal advice, as does telling the employee not to worry about his past fraudulent conduct. As discussed in C, the attorney is not the employee's lawyer. Thus, he should not be giving legal advice to the employee.

46. A is the correct answer. This question illustrates that occasionally the MPRE will test case law that interprets the Model Rules. This question tests your understanding of Rule 1.13, Corporation as a Client. Under Rule 1.13, a lawyer for the corporation has a duty to represent the corporation as a client. The other rule implicated by this question is Rule 1.6—concerning which *Upjohn v. United States* interpreted the attorney-client privilege to cover the corporation as the client. A is correct because the interview was conducted as a confidential communication between Lucas, the corporation's lawyer, and Janitor Jones, an employee of the corporation.

    B is incorrect because the reasoning is not correct and does not refer to a rule.

    C is incorrect because the U.S. Supreme Court in *Upjohn* did not narrow its decision to include a corporate privilege that only applied to higher-level corporate employees; the privilege covers even the janitor.

    D is incorrect because Jones does not have to consent.

47. C is the correct answer. Although receiving property as advance payment of fees from a client is not preferred, it is acceptable if it is kept separate from the property of the attorney. Putting the property in a client-only safe deposit box is the ideal method. See Rule 1.15, Comment [1]. Here, the lawyer received a $10,000 watch as a fee advance. The

lawyer must therefore put the watch in a client-only safe deposit box.

A is incorrect because an attorney can accept an advance payment of fees. But the lawyer may neither wear the watch nor give it to his girlfriend (or anyone else); he must keep it in a client-only safe deposit box.

B is incorrect because a problem will arise if less money is earned than the value of the watch.

D is incorrect because an attorney can accept a watch as advanced fees as long as the attorney does not wear it, etc., and places it in the client-only safe deposit box.

48. D is the correct answer. Under Rule 1.7, a conflict of interest between two concurrent clients can only occur if both clients waive the conflict, in writing, before the representation begins. (Note that in many states, representing two adverse parties in a divorce would be un-waivable). Here, the best answer is D because Alex must obtain a waiver before the representation. He waited too long.

    A is incorrect because there is a substantial relationship between the divorce case and business representation.

    B is incorrect because Alex still violated the rules, even if Winona did consent.

    C is incorrect because it is possible to waive divorce conflicts in some situations.

49. A is the correct answer. Under Rule 1.6, a lawyer has a duty of confidentiality to a client with regard to all information concerning the representation. Here, the question tests the unique situation of insurance counsel for the client—also called the insured—and the duty of the lawyer to represent the client. Even when the lawyer is being paid by the insurance company, the lawyer owes a duty of confidentiality to the insured, the client.

    B is incorrect because there is no designation between primary and secondary client. The only client is Ivan, the insured.

C is incorrect because keeping the information confidential is not defrauding the insurance company. The insurance company has an independent obligation and opportunity to investigate its own facts concerning any coverage issues.

D is incorrect because Ivan was not charged with a crime.

50. A is the correct answer. That the client is not injured is irrelevant to the rule prohibiting commingling, Rule 1.15. Since taking the client's funds was without consent, it is commingling. (Note that this answer would be different if the question dealt, instead, with a malpractice suit by the client against the lawyer. In that case, the client would not prevail because he was not harmed. However, the Model Rules, which deal only with discipline of lawyers, do not care about harm or lack of harm to the client.)

    B is incorrect because lawyers are permitted to gamble with their own money outside of their practice of law.

    C is incorrect because under Rule 1.15, there can be no commingling of funds.

    D is correct because under Rule 1.15, there can be no commingling of funds.

51. B is the correct answer. When the attorney left his fee in the client trust account, this constituted commingling, which is prohibited under Rule 1.15.

    A is incorrect because harm to the client is irrelevant when there is commingling. (Note that this answer would be different if the question dealt, instead, with a malpractice suit by the client against the lawyer. In that case, the client would not prevail because he was not harmed. However, the Model Rules, which deal only with discipline of lawyers, do not care about harm or lack of harm to the client.)

    C is incorrect because lawyers are permitted to try to minimize their tax liability, as long as they do it legally.

    D is incorrect because lawyers are not required to close their trust accounts when they conclude cases; they should keep the trust account open for use in the next case(s).

52. B is the correct answer. Because the attorney-client relationship is fiduciary in nature and because it is the client who is in the position of trust, clients are generally permitted to terminate the services of their attorneys "at will" with little or no penalty. Rule 1.16(a)(3). Attorneys, when terminated, as a general rule, must withdraw; thus, when the client terminates the lawyer, the lawyer must withdraw, regardless of the reason for the termination.

    A is incorrect because the attorney must withdraw (it is not optional).

    C is incorrect because the attorney must withdraw.

    D is incorrect because there is no need for arbitration as to whether the attorney must withdraw after being fired by the client. The lawyer must withdraw, as discussed in B.

53. D is the correct answer. Attorneys must not either harass an opposing party or pursue a frivolous argument. Rule 3.1. Since it is stipulated that the attorney merely desired to "wear down" the opposing party, such action is definitely prohibited.

    A is incorrect because attorneys cannot harass other parties under Rule 3.1.

    B is incorrect because attorneys cannot harass other parties under Rule 3.1.

    C is incorrect because attorneys cannot harass other parties under Rule 3.1.

54. A is the correct answer. The lawyer is not required to alert the judge to any of these authorities because none is binding on the jurisdiction in which the court sits. Rule 3.3(a)(2) concerns a lawyer's duty to alert the court to adverse legal authorities. In Option I, the U.S. Supreme Court case is adverse only by analogy between the State X statute and the federal Lanham Act. Further, the U.S. Supreme Court's interpretation of federal law is not controlling on a State X judge who is applying State X law. For the same reasons, the U.S. Court of Appeals case in Option II need not be disclosed. Further, the State Y case in Option III need not be disclosed because it is adverse only by analogy between

trespass to real property and infringement of a trademark. There may be sound tactical reasons for counsel for Noxatox to use these cases—but the rules do not compel it.

B is incorrect because it does not contain all of the correct option choices, which A does.

C is incorrect because it does not contain all of the correct option choices, which A does.

D is incorrect because it does not contain all of the correct option choices, which A does.

55. B is the correct answer. Attorneys must reveal cases within the jurisdiction that are directly on point. Rule 3.3(a)(2). (Note that there is no requirement to reveal contra cases in California.) Furthermore, attorneys must not purposely mislead the jury in closing argument. Rule 3.3(a)(1). Here, the attorney both failed to reveal a case in the jurisdiction that was directly on point and, in closing argument, alluded to facts that were not offered in the case in chief, which seems to have been done in an attempt to mislead the jury. ("She believes she can 'get this by' the inattentive and ill-informed jury.")

    A is incorrect because attorneys are generally not disciplined for simply losing cases. There must be another factor, such as neglect.

    C is incorrect because attorneys need not reveal cases on point that are outside the jurisdiction, such as the State Q case. (The lawyer's case takes place in State P.)

    D is incorrect because, while attorneys must reveal cases within the jurisdiction that are directly on point, this is only required to be done on the record in court. There is no rule that requires lawyers to inform opposing counsel off the record prior to court.

56. A is the correct answer. An attorney must not help a client commit perjury. Rule 3.3(a)(3). Because the attorney did this, she is subject to discipline. For an attorney to be civilly liable for malpractice, two elements must occur: 1) an attorney error (usually shown by referring to the State's code of ethics) and 2) harm/damages to the client. Because

the client was acquitted, the second element is missing, and there is no malpractice liability.

B is incorrect because an attorney cannot help a client commit perjury.

C is incorrect because an attorney cannot help a client commit perjury.

D is incorrect because an attorney cannot help a client commit perjury.

57. C is the correct answer. Rule 1.15 directs that a lawyer must keep all client money in the Client Trust Account. An attorney cannot remove client money for any reason. C is correct because Lee could have paid the amount out of her personal account so that no client money was used. Further, under Rule 1.8(e), a lawyer is permitted to advance litigation costs.

A is incorrect because Lee's handling of the matter was improper.

B is incorrect because Lee would not have been subject to sanctions for allowing Watkins to go to jail. She could choose to pay the fine, but she was not obligated to do so.

D is not correct because Lee misappropriated funds.

58. A is the correct answer. Attorneys enjoy First Amendment free-speech protection. Thus, they are permitted to speak to the press pre-trial. Attorneys can be disciplined only if they know or reasonably should know that there is a substantial likelihood that their comments will prejudice the trial. See generally Rule 3.6. Here, since the attorney's conduct fell short of that standard (since he was merely trying to motivate the other side to settle), the conduct was proper.

B is incorrect because attorney speech is protected by the First Amendment, although they cannot make comments that will prejudice the trial.

C is incorrect because attorney speech is protected by the First Amendment, although they cannot make comments that will prejudice the trial.

D is incorrect because attorney speech is protected by the First Amendment, although they cannot make comments that will prejudice the trial.

59. A is the correct answer. A lawyer is permitted to testify as to the value of her legal services. Rule 3.7(a) (2).

    B is incorrect because the lawyer can testify regarding the value of her legal services.

    C is incorrect because the lawyer can testify regarding the value of her legal services.

    D is incorrect because the lawyer can testify regarding the value of her legal services.

60. D is the correct answer. A lawyer must not communicate with a represented party, unless the lawyer has the consent of the other lawyer or is authorized to do so by law or a court order. Rule 4.2. Here, there was no consent by the woman's attorney for the man's lawyer to contact the woman directly, nor was there a court order.

    A is incorrect because a lawyer cannot communicate with a represented party under Rule 4.2.

    B is incorrect a lawyer cannot communicate with a represented party under Rule 4.2.

    C is incorrect because a lawyer cannot communicate with a represented party under Rule 4.2.

MPRE Simulated Exam 2

1. Attorney represented Plaintiff in litigation that was settled, with Plaintiff's approval, for $25,000. Attorney received a check in that amount from Defendant, payable to Attorney's order. Attorney endorsed and deposited the check in Attorney's Clients' Trust Account. Attorney promptly notified Plaintiff and billed Plaintiff $5,000 for legal fees. Plaintiff disputed the amount of the fee and wrote Attorney, stating, "I will agree to pay $3,000 as a reasonable fee for the work you did, but I will not pay anything more than that."

   It is proper for Attorney to:

   I. Retain the entire $25,000 in Attorney's Clients' Trust Account until the fee dispute is settled.

   II. Send Plaintiff $20,000, transfer $3,000 to Attorney's office account, and retain $2,000 in Attorney's Clients' Trust Account until the dispute is settled.

   III. Send Plaintiff $20,000 and transfer $5,000 to Attorney's office account.

   A. I and II, but not III.

   B. I only.

   C. I, II, and III.

   D. II only.

2. Attorney represents Client, a famous politician in an action against Newspaper for libel. The case has attracted substantial publicity, and a jury trial has been demanded. After one of the pretrial hearings, as Attorney left the courthouse, news reporters interviewed Attorney. In responding to questions, Attorney truthfully stated: "The judge has upheld our right to subpoena the reporter involved (identified in our motion as Jane Doe) and question her on her mental impressions when she prepared the article." Is Attorney subject to discipline for making this statement?

A. No, because the trial has not commenced.

B. Yes, because Attorney identified a prospective witness in the case.

C. No, because the statement relates to a matter of public record.

D. Yes, because prospective jurors might learn of Attorney's remarks.

3. Defendant was on trial for the murder of Victim, who was killed during a bar brawl. In the course of closing arguments to the jury, Prosecutor said, "Defendant's entire defense is based on the testimony of Wit, who said that Victim attacked Defendant with a knife before Defendant struck him. No other witness testified to such an attack by Victim. I don't believe Wit was telling the truth, and I don't think you believe him either." Was Prosecutor's statement proper?

A. No, because Prosecutor alluded to the beliefs of the jurors.

B. Yes, if Prosecutor accurately stated the testimony in the case.

C. No, because Prosecutor asserted his personal opinion about Wit's credibility.

D. Yes, if Prosecutor, in fact, believed Wit was lying.

4. Attorney represents Client, the plaintiff in a civil action that was filed a year ago and is about to be set for trial. Client informed Attorney that he could be available at any time during the months of October, November, and December. In discussing possible trial dates with opposing counsel and the court clerk, Attorney was advised that a trial date on October 5 was available and that the next available trial date would be December 10. Without first consulting Client, Attorney requested the December 10 trial date because she was representing Deft, the defendant in a felony criminal trial that was set for October 20 and she wanted as much time as possible to prepare for that trial. Was it proper for Attorney to agree to the December trial date without obtaining Client's consent?

A. Yes, because a criminal trial takes precedence over a civil trial.

B. No, because Attorney should manage her calendar so that her cases can be tried promptly.

C. No, unless Attorney was court-appointed counsel in the criminal case.

D. Yes, unless Client will be prejudiced by the delay.

5. Jeff represented Carl in a property dispute against Adam. The trial court ruled in favor of Carl. Adam decided to appeal. Both Carl and Adam decided to get different lawyers. In the meantime, Jeff was hired at Smith & Smith. Adam decided to hire Bonny, who also works at Smith & Smith. Who may work on the case?

A. Neither Bonny nor Jeff.

B. Only Jeff.

C. Both Jeff and Bonny because Jeff will give Adam an advantage and the firm is obligated to take the advantage.

D. Bonny, if Jeff is not allowed to participate in the case and Smith & Smith inform Carl of the steps taken to prevent Jeff from participating in the case.

6. Lawyer was extremely busy and had a very skillful paralegal on her staff. Lawyer was heading to trial and asked her paralegal to draft a client's answers to various discovery requests. Paralegal completed the project and texted Lawyer to ask whether paralegal should send the answers off to opposing counsel. Lawyer texted back: "Yes, please send ASAP." Did Lawyer violate the ethical rules?

A. No, because Lawyer knew that her paralegal was competent.

B. No, because there was an important discovery deadline that was important to client's case.

C. Yes, because Lawyer was required to supervise paralegal's work even if paralegal was competent.

D. Yes, because Lawyer failed to be diligent in getting the discovery answers completed in a timely fashion.

7. An attorney represented a client in an action against the client's former business partner to recover damages for breach of contract. During the representation, the client presented the attorney with incontrovertible proof that the partner had committed perjury in a prior action that was resolved in the partner's favor. Neither the attorney nor the client was involved in any way in the prior action. The attorney believes that it would be detrimental to the client's best interests to reveal the perjury because implications might be drawn from the former close personal and business relationship between the client and the partner. Is it proper for the attorney to disclose the perjury to the tribunal?

   A. No, because the attorney believes that the disclosure would be detrimental to the client's best interests.

   B. No, because neither the client nor the attorney was involved in the prior action.

   C. Yes, because the attorney has knowledge that the partner perpetrated a fraud on the tribunal.

   D. Yes, because the information is unprivileged.

8. An attorney represented a plaintiff in a civil suit against a defendant who was also represented by a lawyer. In the course of developing the plaintiff's case, the attorney discovered evidence that she reasonably believed showed that the defendant had committed a crime. The attorney felt that the defendant's crime should be reported to local prosecutorial authorities. After full disclosure, the plaintiff consented to the attorney's doing so. Without advising the defendant's lawyer, the attorney informed the local prosecutor of her findings, but she sought no advantage in the civil suit from her actions. The defendant was subsequently indicted, tried, and acquitted of the offense. Was the attorney's disclosure to prosecutorial authorities proper?

   A. Yes, because the attorney reasonably believed that the defendant had committed a crime.

B. Yes, because the attorney was required to report unprivileged knowledge of criminal conduct.

C. No, because the attorney did not know that the defendant had committed a crime.

D. No, because the plaintiff's civil suit against the defendant was still pending.

9. An attorney who had represented a client for many years prepared the client's will and acted as one of the two subscribing witnesses to its execution. The will gave 10% of the client's estate to the client's housekeeper, 10% to the client's son and sole heir, and the residue to charity. Upon the client's death one year later, the executor named in the will asked the attorney to represent him in probating the will and administering the estate. At that time, the executor informed the attorney that the son had notified him that he would contest the probate of the will on the grounds that the client lacked the required mental capacity at the time the will was executed. The attorney believes that the client was fully competent at all times and will so testify if called as a witness. The other subscribing witness to the client's will predeceased the client. Is it proper for the attorney to represent the executor in the probate of the will?

   A. Yes, because the attorney is the sole surviving witness to the execution of the will.

   B. Yes, because the attorney's testimony will support the validity of the will.

   C. No, because the attorney will be called to testify on a contested issue of fact.

   D. No, because the attorney will be representing an interest adverse to the interests of the client's heir.

10. Carl, a certified public accountant, has proposed to Attorney, a recognized specialist in the field of tax law, that Carl and Attorney form a partnership to provide clients with tax-related legal and accounting services. Both Carl and Attorney have deserved reputations of being competent, honest, and trustworthy. Carl further proposes that the announcement of the proposed partnership, the firm

stationery, and all public directory listings clearly state that Carl is a certified public accountant and that Attorney is a lawyer. Is Attorney subject to discipline if he enters into the proposed partnership with Carl?

A. No, because the partnership will assure to the public high-quality services in the fields of tax law and accounting.

B. Yes, because Attorney would be receiving fees paid for other than legal services.

C. Yes, because one of the activities of the partnership would be providing legal services to clients.

D. No, if Attorney is the only person in the partnership who gives advice on legal matters.

11. Attorney represents Bank in its commercial loan transactions. Corp has applied to Bank for a loan of $900,000 to be secured by a lien on Corp's inventory. The inventory, consisting of small items, constantly turns over. The security documents are complex and if improperly drawn could result in an invalid lien. Bank has approved the loan on the condition that Attorney prepare the necessary security instruments and that Corp pay Attorney's fees. This arrangement is customary in the city in which Attorney's law office and Bank are located. It is obvious to Attorney that he can adequately represent the interests of both Corp and Bank. After Corp and Bank consulted with other lawyers, each consented in writing to the representation. Is it proper for Attorney to prepare the security documents under these circumstances?

A. Yes, because the arrangement is customary in the community.

B. No, because Attorney's fees are being paid by Corp, not Bank.

C. No, because Corp and Bank have differing interests.

D. Yes, because Bank and Corp have given their informed consent to the arrangement.

12. Attorney represented Plaintiff in Plaintiff's action for defamation against Defendant. After Defendant's lawyer had filed and served an answer, Attorney, at Plaintiff's direction, hired PI, a licensed private investigator, and instructed PI to attempt to interview Defendant without revealing his employment with Attorney. PI succeeded in interviewing Defendant privately and obtained an admission from Defendant that the statements Defendant had made were based solely on unsubstantiated gossip. Is Attorney subject to discipline for obtaining the statement from Defendant in this matter?

    A. No, because Attorney was following Plaintiff's instructions.

    B. No, because the statement obtained was evidence that Defendant's allegations were unfounded.

    C. Yes, because Attorney instructed PI to interview Defendant.

    D. Yes, because Attorney should have interviewed Defendant personally.

13. Attorney, representing Client and with Client's approval, settled a claim against Defendant for $60,000. The settlement agreement provided that one-half would be paid by Insco, Defendant's primary insurance carrier, and one-half by Sureco, a co-insurer. Attorney's agreed-upon fee was 30% of the amount of the settlement. Attorney received Insco's check for $30,000 and a letter from Sureco advising that its check would be sent in two weeks. Attorney promptly advised Client and deposited the $30,000 in her Clients' Trust Account. Client demanded that Attorney send him the entire $30,000 and take her fee out of the funds to be received from Sureco. Which of the following would now be proper for Attorney?

    I. Send Client $30,000.

    II. Send Client $21,000 and retain $9,000 in Attorney's Clients' Trust Account.

    III. Send Client $21,000 and transfer $9,000 to her personal account.

A. I, II, and III.

B. I only.

C. I and II, but not III.

D. I and III, but not II.

14. Attorney represents Driver, the plaintiff in an automobile accident case. Two weeks before the date set for trial, Attorney discovered that Witt was an eyewitness to the accident. Attorney interviewed Witt. Witt's version of the accident was contrary to that of Driver and, if believed by the trier of fact, would establish that Driver was at fault. Witt told Attorney that she had not been interviewed by defense counsel. Witt also told Attorney that she intended to leave for Europe the following week for a one-month vacation unless she had an obligation to remain and attend the trial. Attorney told Witt: "No one has subpoenaed you yet. You have no legal duty to make yourself available. Trials can be difficult affairs. Witnesses sometimes get very nervous because of the questions asked by the lawyers. Why don't you take the vacation as planned, and, by the time you return, the trial will be over." Is Attorney subject to discipline?

A. Yes, because Attorney did not subpoena Witt despite knowing she was an eyewitness.

B. Yes, because Attorney advised Witt even though Attorney was not Witt's lawyer.

C. No, because Attorney did not offer Witt any inducement not to appear at the trial.

D. No, because Witt had not been subpoenaed by the defense.

15. Carrie alleges that she was assaulted by Donald, a very wealthy congressman. Carrie contacted lawyer Lennie about representing her in a civil action against Donald. After several lengthy discussions about the merits of the case, Carrie decided to employ attorney Albert to represent her instead. Donald was later charged with criminal assault in connection with this incident, and his trial was televised. Lennie watched the trial and was astonished when Carrie

testified to facts that Lennie knew from their previous discussions to be false. Lennie sent a letter with a messenger over to the court to notify the court that Carrie had perjured herself. Were Lennie's actions proper?

A. No, unless he sent copies of the letter to the prosecution and defense attorneys and they were given an opportunity to respond.

B. No, because Lennie's information was gained during his discussions with Carrie.

C. Yes, because his actions were necessary to prevent Carrie from perpetrating a fraud on the court.

D. Yes, because Carrie committed a criminal act by testifying falsely.

16. Lawyer Albert was licensed to practice in the State of California. He often works in association with Bonnie on a temporary basis regarding legal matters in the State of Texas. Bonnie is also licensed to practice in Texas. Albert was recently disbarred in California. Bonnie recently asked Albert to help her with a case in Texas. Albert agreed, and they won the case. Assuming Texas follows the Model Rules, is Albert subject to discipline?

A. No, because he is licensed in Texas.

B. Yes, because he was disbarred in California.

C. No, because he worked in association with Bonnie, who is licensed in Texas.

D. Yes, but only if the case was in relation to a case he worked on in California before he was disbarred.

17. Attorney wants to make it easier for her clients to pay their bills for her fees. Which of the following moves by Attorney would be proper?

I. Accept bank credit cards in payment of Attorney's fees.

II. Arrange for clients to obtain bank loans for the purpose of paying Attorney's fees.

III. If a case is interesting, suggest that the client give Attorney publication rights concerning the case as partial payment of the fee.

A. II only.

B. I and II, but not III.

C. I, II, and III.

D. Neither I, II, nor III.

18. Attorney is employed by Client, who is a fugitive under indictment for burglary. After thorough legal research and investigation of the facts furnished by Client, Attorney reasonably came to believe that the indictment is fatally defective and should be dismissed as a matter of law. Attorney advised Client of his opinion and urged Client to turn herself in. Client told attorney she would not do so. Attorney advised the District Attorney that he represented Client and that he had counseled her to surrender, but she refused to follow his advice. Attorney has not advised Client on how to avoid arrest and prosecution, and does not know where she is hiding.

Is Attorney subject to discipline if he continues to represent the client?

A. Yes, because the client is engaging in continuing illegal conduct.

B. Yes, because the client refused to accept Attorney's advice to surrender.

C. No, because Attorney is not counseling the client to avoid arrest and prosecution.

D. No, because Attorney reasonably believes the indictment is defective.

19. A state law forbids drivers under the age of 18 to drive after 8:00 p.m. Failure to comply is a misdemeanor punishable by a $150 fine. Attorney is hired by a minor and his parent, who asked if any people have been prosecuted under the law, and whether the fine could be imposed each time the minor drives after 8:00 p.m., or only once. The minor and his parent also asked what the minor could do to minimize his

risk of detection if he broke this law. Attorney told them that nobody had been prosecuted under the law, and accurately told the client that the fine could be imposed only once, rather than for each incident of a minor driving after 8:00 p.m. Attorney also told the minor and his parent that she thought it was improper to advise them as to how best avoid detection while breaking this law. The minor and his parent thanked Attorney, and several weeks later, Attorney found out that the minor had begun driving after 8:00 p.m. in violation of the state law.

Is Attorney subject to discipline?

A. Yes, because Attorney reasonably should have known that the info she gave would encourage the minor to violate the law.

B. Yes, because Attorney did not discourage the minor from breaking the law.

C. No, because Attorney merely gave her honest opinion of consequences that could happen if the minor broke the law.

D. No, because Attorney and the minor could have discussed the best way to avoid detection under the law.

20. An attorney represents a litigation client in a matter scheduled to go to trial in 5 months. Recently, the client has disagreed with almost all of the attorney's tactical decisions. The attorney said to the client, "If you don't like the way I am running your representation, maybe you should find a new attorney." The client was upset and believed the attorney was trying to get out of the representation. Reasonably believing he could no longer work effectively with the client, the attorney sought the client's permission to withdraw, and the client reluctantly agreed. After giving the client sufficient notice to obtain replacement counsel, the attorney requested the court's permission to withdraw, but the court denied the request.

Is the attorney permitted to withdraw from the representation?

A. No, because the court denied the attorney's request to withdraw.

B. Yes, because the client agreed, and the attorney gave the client sufficient notice to obtain replacement counsel before the trial was set to begin.

C. Yes, because the client had made it unreasonably difficult for the attorney to carry out the representation effectively.

D. No, because the attorney's withdrawal would cause material prejudice to the client, and the client's agreement was not voluntary.

21. Attorney filed an action for breach of fiduciary duty on behalf of client. In fact, the client had no legal basis for the suit, but wanted to harass the defendant. To induce the attorney to file the action, the client made certain false statements of material fact to the attorney, which the attorney included in the complaint. The attorney did not know of the falsity of the statements when he filed the complaint on behalf of the client. At trial, the client took the stand and testified as set forth in the complaint, and the client won. After entry of judgment, the client sent a letter to the attorney which was marked "for your eyes only" and in which the client admitted that she had falsely testified and lied to the attorney. The defendant contacted the state bar and claimed that the attorney had knowingly used false testimony in the case. Disciplinary proceedings were instituted against the attorney.

Is it proper for the attorney to use the client's letter in the attorney's defense in the disciplinary proceedings?

A. Yes, because the client had committed a fraud on the court in which the case was tried.

B. No, because the attorney learned the facts from the client in confidence.

C. Yes, if it is necessary to do so to protect the attorney's rights.

D. No, if disclosure by the attorney could result in the client's prosecution for perjury.

22. Attorney represented a client in a matter that was settled before a complaint was filed. The settlement proceeds were paid directly to the client, who then paid the attorney in full for her fees and expenses. The attorney did not do any further work for the client. The client is now being investigated by the FBI in connection with the matter handled by the attorney on behalf of the client. The FBI has informally asked the attorney for details of the settlement, including the amount claimed for each item of damage and the amounts paid for the items. The attorney reported the request to the client, who told her not to provide the information to the FBI.

    Is it proper for the attorney to provide the information to the FBI?

    A. Yes, if the information does not involve the attorney's work product.

    B. No, because the client told the attorney not to provide the information.

    C. Yes, because the attorney no longer represents the client.

    D. No, unless the attorney believes the disclosure would benefit the client.

23. Attorney Aiden regularly represents Dinomac, a microwave parts manufacturer. One morning the president of Dinomac called Aiden and said excitedly, "Have you heard the news reports about children getting their fingers snapped off in microwave doors? Journalists are saying the microwaves were all made in the last 5 years, and I'm almost positive those doors were made with Dinomac parts. I looked through records in our system and saw that some of our microwave door parts were not tested before distribution. These records are fairly old and should be shredded. I'm going to shred them now unless you tell me otherwise."

Must Aiden advise the president to keep the records?

A. No, because at this point there is no litigation pending against the company respecting this matter.

B. Yes, because the records have potential evidentiary value if the company gets sued.

C. No, unless it is certain that the company was the manufacturer of the dishwasher in question.

D. Yes, unless the company has a clearly-established policy of shredding quality control records after two years.

24. Attorney Anton represented Billy Buyer in a real estate transaction. Due to Anton's professional negligence in drafting the sales agreement, Billy was required to pay for an inspection that should have been paid for by the other party to the transaction. Attorney Anton recognized the mistake and told Billy about his error. After a discussion about the mistake, Billy told Anton he would accept repayment of the inspection fees from Anton as settlement of any potential negligence claim Billy might have against Anton related to the error. Although Billy might have recovered additional damages if he had filed a malpractice action, Attorney Anton reasonably believed that the proposed settlement was fair to Billy. Anton readily agreed to make the reimbursement so as to avoid a malpractice action by Billy. He drafted a settlement agreement and both he and Billy executed it. Was Attorney Anton's conduct proper?

A. No, because Attorney Anton settled a case involving liability for malpractice while the matter was still ongoing.

B. No, unless Billy was separately represented in negotiating and finalizing the settlement agreement.

C. Yes, if Attorney Anton advised Billy in writing that Billy should seek independent legal representation before deciding to enter into the settlement agreement.

D. Yes, because Attorney Anton reasonably believed that the proposed settlement was fair to Billy.

25. Millionaire actress Cara Casa dies unexpectedly of a drug overdose, leaving her entire fortune to her infant daughter Laura. Cara was married to Defendant Daniel at the time Laura was born. Under applicable law, Daniel is presumed to be Cara's father, but that presumption can be rebutted by a DNA test ordered pursuant to a parentage case. Plaintiff Peter has come forward and claimed a long-time affair with Cara, and claims that he is Laura's father. Laura's father will exercise control over the child's now substantial fortune. Plaintiff Peter has hired Attorney Alice to file a paternity action on his behalf. The matter has attracted substantial media attention, and as soon as Alice files the action, she is surrounded by reporters seeking a comment. The reporters sought her comment before any other attorney's comment in the matter. Which of the following statements, if believed by Alice to be true, would be proper for her to make?

I. "As stated in our pleadings, we believe that a DNA test will prove conclusively that Peter is the father of Laura."

II. "Cara was no longer in love with Daniel by the time Laura was conceived."

III. "We have been unable to locate several people whose testimony will be helpful to us, and we implore them to contact us immediately."

A. II only.

B. III only.

C. I and III, but not II.

D. I, II, and III.

26. Lawyer Louis is one of the top communications lawyers in the country. The federal government announces that a limited number of new broadcast licenses will be made available next year. Two major broadcasting companies, CNNC and KBCJ, separately contact Louis and ask him to represent them in their applications for one of the new licenses. Though in some sense, the two companies will be competing for one of the limited number of licenses, Louis is

confident that he can adequately represent each in their applications. May Louis represent both companies?

A. Yes, as long as each gives informed written consent and agrees to waive any actual and potential conflicts that may arise from the representation.

B. Yes, provided that each agrees to waive their right of confidentiality owed to them by Louis.

C. No, because the companies' interests are directly adverse in relation to obtaining a license.

D. No, because a lawyer owes each of his clients a duty of loyalty.

27. Plaintiff Penny is suing her former employer Malco for wrongful termination. On cross-examination, Malco's lawyer asks Penny if she ever came to work under the influence of alcohol after March 31, 2009. The parties agree that Penny came to work drunk on March 31, 2009. Penny answers "no." While the answer is literally true, Penny's lawyer Larry knows that Penny in fact went to work under the influence of a number of other drugs besides alcohol on dates after March 31, 2009. Must Larry disclose to the tribunal the fact that Penny appeared for work under the influence of drugs other than alcohol after March 31, 2009?

A. No, because an attorney owes a paramount duty of confidentiality to their client.

B. Yes, because an attorney owes a duty of candor to the tribunal.

C. No, because Penny's testimony was literally true.

D. Yes, because an attorney must take remedial measures if the attorney reasonably believes the tribunal will draw a false inference from the evidence presented.

28. Brothers Bobby and Benji are charged with robbery of a gas station and non-capital felony murder because the cashier was shot and killed during the robbery. It is alleged that Bobby committed the robbery and killing while Benji waited outside in their car. In fact, the evidence showing that Benji was a knowing participant in the crime is extremely weak.

The Brothers want Attorney Alpha to represent them jointly, and are willing to waive any conflicts of interest. Alpha expects the D.A. to offer leniency to Benji in exchange for Benji's testimony against Bobby. May Alpha represent both Bobby and Benji concurrently?

A. No, because Alpha cannot reasonably believe that he can represent adequately the interests of both brothers in these circumstances.

B. No, because the rules prohibit joint representation in such circumstances.

C. Yes, unless the brothers' testimony will be directly conflicting.

D. Yes, because the brothers are willing to waive any conflicts of interest.

29. Attorney Adam represented Husband Harry and Wife Wilma in setting up their family restaurant business. During the course of the representation, Adam became highly familiar with the personal financial circumstances of both Harry and Wilma. Running the business has put a strain on the couple's marriage, and Harry and Wilma decide to divorce. Wilma is served with a divorce petition from Harry. After reading the petition, Wilma notices that Adam is already representing Harry in the divorce case. Angry, Wilma calls Harry to complain. A short time later, Wilma receives a letter from Adam asking her to consent in writing to his representation of Harry in the divorce proceedings. Wilma reluctantly agrees. Has Adam acted properly?

A. Yes, because there is no substantial relationship between the divorce case and the business representation.

B. Yes, because he obtained a conflict waiver from Wilma.

C. No, because Adam did not have the waiver notarized.

D. No, because Wilma's conflict waiver was requested after the representation had already begun.

30. When attorney Hodges graduated from law school three years ago, she opened a solo practice in a small rural community close to the state's major prison. Her primary interests were family law and real estate law. Her practice is growing very slowly, despite her long work hours. She is barely able to make financial ends meet. The presiding judge of the local State District Court has asked her to serve as court-appointed counsel in a civil action that was originally filed *pro se* by an indigent inmate of the prison. From the roughly drawn complaint, the presiding judge believes there may be some merit in the inmate's allegations of brutality by some of the guards and gross neglect on the part of the warden. State law allows attorney fees to be awarded to a plaintiff in a civil action of this type, but only if the plaintiff is victorious. Attorney Hodges realizes that she will not be paid for her work if she loses the case, and she is very concerned about the financial loss she may suffer if she takes time away from her regular practice. Further, she is worried about harming her reputation because the warden and many prison employees form the nucleus of her community. Which of the following statements are correct?

    I. She may decline to serve on the ground that her practice is primarily in the fields of real estate and family law.

    II. She may decline to serve if she believes in good faith that she cannot reasonably take the financial risk involved.

    III. She may decline to serve if she believes in good faith that to serve would seriously injure her reputation in the community.

    IV. She may decline to serve if she believes in good faith that some of her present clients will be offended if she takes the case.

    A. All of the above.

    B. None of the above.

    C. II only.

    D. I, II, and IV only.

31. Lawyer Linda is admitted to practice in State A, but not in State B. Her cousin asks her to write a letter recommending him for admission to practice law in State B. Linda knows that her cousin is educationally well-qualified to be a lawyer, but she regards him as thoroughly dishonest. May Linda write a letter stating that her cousin is fit to practice law and has an honest moral character?

    A. No, because Linda is not a member of the bar of State B.

    B. No, because Linda would be making a false statement of a material fact.

    C. Yes, because her belief about her cousin's lack of honesty is merely her own opinion.

    D. Yes, because the bar of State B will decide for itself whether her cousin is a person of good moral character.

32. Attorney has been hired by Client to represent Client in a civil commitment proceeding initiated by the State. Client is now undergoing psychiatric evaluation to determine whether civil commitment should be ordered. Client told Attorney that Client intends to commit suicide as soon as the tests are completed, and Attorney believes that Client will carry out this threat. Suicide and attempted suicide are crimes in the state. Is it proper for Attorney to disclose Client's intentions to the authorities?

    A. Yes, because the information concerns a future crime that is likely to result in substantial bodily harm including Client's imminent death.

    B. Yes, because the information concerns a future crime and is not protected by the attorney-client evidentiary privilege.

    C. No, unless Attorney knows that client has attempted suicide in the past.

    D. No, because disclosure would aid the state in its civil commitment case against Client.

33. For many years, Attorney has served as outside counsel to Corp, a corporation. Shortly after a change in management,

Attorney discovered what she reasonably believed to be a material misstatement in a document she had drafted that Attorney was about to file on Corp's behalf with a government agency. Attorney advised Corp's Board of Directors that filing the document was probably criminal. However, the Board disagreed that there was any material misstatement and directed Attorney to proceed with the filing. When Attorney indicated her intention to resign, Corp argued that a resignation at this time would send a signal that there was a problem with the filing. Corp urged Attorney to continue the representation, but offered to use in-house counsel to complete the work on the filing. Although she does not know for certain that filing the document is illegal, Attorney reasonably believes that it is. In any event, Attorney is personally uncomfortable with the representation and wants to withdraw. May Attorney withdraw from her representation of Corp?

A. Yes, because withdrawal is permitted but not required when a client insists on conduct which the lawyer reasonably believes, but does not know, will be criminal.

B. Yes, because withdrawal is required when a client insists on conduct which the lawyer reasonably believes, but does not know, will be criminal.

C. No, if Corp is correct that withdrawal would breach confidentiality by sending a signal that the filing is problematic.

D. No, if Attorney's withdrawal as outside counsel might affect Corp's ability to complete the filing in a timely fashion.

34. Attorney Alpha, a partner in the law firm of Alpha & Beta, was retained by Mary, the plaintiff in a personal injury action against Deft. The jury rendered a verdict in favor of Deft, and Alpha filed an appeal on Mary's behalf. Alpha reviewed the trial transcript and wrote the brief. The brief stated, "It is uncontroverted that Deft failed to signal before turning left into the intersection." In fact, Wit, a witness called by Deft, testified that Deft did signal before turning. Alpha was aware of this testimony, having read it while

reviewing the trial transcript. Three days before the appeal was scheduled to be argued in the state's intermediate appellate court, Alpha suffered a heart attack. Attorney Beta, one of Alpha's partners, agreed to argue the appeal. Beta knew nothing about the case and had no opportunity to confer with Alpha. In preparing for the argument, Beta read Alpha's brief thoroughly and read as much of the trial transcript as was possible in the limited time available, but did not read Wit's testimony. In oral argument, Beta stated to the court, "Your honors, as stated in our brief, it is uncontroverted that Deft failed to signal before turning left into the intersection." Beta assumed that Alpha's statement in the brief to that effect was correct. Is Beta subject to discipline for making this statement during oral argument?

A. Yes, because the statement was false.

B. Yes, because Beta did not know whether or not the statement was true.

C. No, because Beta did not know that the statement was false.

D. No, because all Beta did was to truthfully recount the statement made by Alpha in the brief.

35. Attorney experienced several instances when clients failed to pay their fees in a timely manner, but it was too late in the representation to withdraw without prejudicing the clients. To avoid a recurrence of this situation, Attorney has drafted a stipulation of consent to her withdrawal if fees are not paid according to the fee agreement. She proposes to have all clients sign the stipulation at the outset of representation. Is it proper for Attorney to use the stipulation to withdraw from representation whenever a client fails to pay fees?

A. Yes, because a lawyer may withdraw when the financial burden of continuing the representation would be substantially greater than the parties anticipated at the time of the fee agreement.

B. Yes, because the client consented to the withdrawal in the stipulation.

C. No, because a client's failure to pay fees when due may be insufficient in itself to justify withdrawal.

D. No, unless clients are provided an opportunity to seek independent legal advice before signing the stipulation.

36. Attorney was retained by Defendant to represent him in a paternity suit. Aunt, Defendant's aunt, believed the suit was unfounded and motivated by malice. Aunt sent Attorney a check for $1,000 and asked Attorney to apply it to the payment of Defendant's fee. Aunt told Attorney not to tell Defendant of the payment because "Defendant is too proud to accept gifts, but I know he really needs the money." Is it proper for Attorney to accept Aunt's check?

A. Yes, if Aunt's goals for the case are the same as Defendant's.

B. Yes, if Attorney's charges to Defendant are reduced accordingly.

C. No, because Aunt is attempting to finance litigation to which she is not a party.

D. No, unless Attorney first informs Defendant and obtains Defendant's consent to retain the payment.

37. Attorney represents Bank in its commercial loan transactions. Corp has applied to Bank for a loan of $900,000 to be secured by a lien on Corp's inventory. The inventory, consisting of small items, constantly turns over. The security documents are complex and if improperly drawn could result in an invalid lien. Bank has approved the loan on the condition that Attorney prepare the necessary security instruments and that Corp pay Attorney's fees. This arrangement is customary in the city in which Attorney's law office and Bank are located. It is obvious to Attorney that he can adequately represent the interests of both Corp and Bank. After Corp and Bank consulted with other lawyers, each consented in writing to the representation. Is it proper for Attorney to prepare the security documents under these circumstances?

A. Yes, because Bank and Corp have given their informed consent to the arrangement.

B. Yes, because the arrangement is customary in the community.

C. No, because Attorney's fees are being paid by Corp, not Bank.

D. No, because Corp and Bank have differing interests.

38. Robber disclosed to his Attorney that Robber robbed the First National Bank of $100,000 in cash. Robber subsequently died in an unrelated accident. Attorney was later called as a witness at the trial of Joe, who had been charged with the robbery committed by Robber. Joe's defense attorney called Attorney to the witness stand and asked him, under oath: "Isn't it true that Robber committed this crime?" Must Attorney assert the Attorney-Client Privilege and refuse to answer the question?

A. No, because Robber is now dead.

B. No, because Joe's interests outweigh Robber's interests.

C. No, because the crime-fraud exception applies here.

D. Yes.

39. Dana is representing Curt in a criminal prosecution. Prior to trial, Curt asks Dana to move to suppress a critical piece of evidence that was seized during Curt's arrest. Dana does not research the issue and does not move to suppress the evidence. In fact, however, it is clear under the law that the evidence should have been suppressed, and a reasonable lawyer would have moved to do so. At trial, the prosecution makes heavy use of the evidence that should have been suppressed. Curt is ultimately acquitted. Soon thereafter, Curt sues Dana for malpractice, and the state seeks to sanction Dana for incompetence. The most likely result is:

A. Dana is found liable for malpractice and sanctioned for incompetence.

B. Dana is found liable for malpractice but not sanctioned for incompetence.

C. Dana is not found liable for malpractice but is sanctioned for incompetence.

D. Dana is not found liable for malpractice and is not sanctioned for incompetence.

40. Attorney represents Client who is the plaintiff in a tort action in state court. Defendant has asserted that Client was contributorily negligent and therefore should be barred from any recovery. In response, Client wants to argue the Last Clear Chance Doctrine. The state's highest court has held that the Last Clear Chance Doctrine is unavailable as an exception to the defense of contributory negligence in this jurisdiction. Will Attorney be subject to professional discipline if Attorney asserts the Last Clear Chance Doctrine?

   A. Yes, because it is contrary to the decision of the state's highest court.

   B. Yes, because were Attorney to assert the exception, she would be acting incompetently.

   C. No, if Attorney can provide a good faith argument for reversal of the applicable law.

   D. No, because Attorney is zealously advancing Client's interests.

41. Judge Jody is a judge in State A. Judge Jody's grandmother, Grandma, lives in State B. Grandma mentioned that she just had her attorney update her will. In lieu of payment, Grandma's attorney, Attorney Annie, put in the will that Annie would receive $10,000 upon the grandmother's death. Grandma told Judge Judy that she was concerned about the larger amount of money that her estate would owe her attorney upon her death. Attorney Annie is admitted to practice in State B. Judge Jody was concerned and wanted contact the State B disciplinary board about Attorney Annie's actions. Is it permissible for Judge Jody to contact State B?

   A. No, because she is not allowed to communicate about facts learned during the course of representation.

   B. No, because legal ethics violations that take place outside State A where she is barred as an attorney are not within her concern.

C. Yes, because she knows that Attorney Annie has violated a legal ethics role.

D. Yes, because she received credible information suggesting that an attorney has violated an ethical rule.

42. Lawyer Lacy, one year out of law school, was assigned a pro bono trial from the Community Lawyer's Network, an organization that refers cases to newer attorneys. The case involved the defense of a teacher for felony child abuse. A few days before trial, Lacy got nervous and believed she was incompetent to actually handle the trial. She filed a motion with the judge for the case requesting to withdraw as counsel. The judge denied her request believing that she was actually quite competent to handle the trial. Lacy nonetheless felt she could not handle the case. She called the client and told the client that he could come pick up his files at any time, but that she could not continue as his lawyer. Is Lacy subject to discipline?

A. No, because she was handling the case pro bono which has different rules for withdrawal.

B. No, because she believed that she was not competent to handle the criminal defense.

C. Yes, because she withdrew from the case right before trial which both violated a judge's order and would severely prejudice the client's case.

D. Yes, because Lacy should have known she was incompetent to handle a criminal defense case given her relatively new status as a lawyer.

43. Attorney Abe's friend was a juror in a criminal matter. One afternoon, Attorney Abe received a call from his friend who was currently presiding as a juror in the criminal trial. His friend asked him the meaning of the term "intent" as it related to a burglary charge. Attorney Abe provided a brief but accurate description of his understanding of "intent" as an element of burglary. Is Attorney Abe subject to discipline?

A. No, unless he specialized in family law and not criminal law.

B. Yes, because it would have been impossible to have provided an accurate description of "intent" in such a short amount of time.

C. No, unless he was related to one of the lawyers or parties in the case.

D. Yes, because Abe talked to a juror who was currently hearing a case which violates Rule 3.5. Lawyers are not permitted to communicate with jurors about cases when a case is pending.

44. David completed law school but he hated every minute of it and decided he did not want to practice law. So David never took the bar examination in his state. Instead, he decided to work as a private investigator for a small law firm, Dudley Law Firm. Which of the following statements are true?

I. David's friend contacted the Dudley Law Firm to represent him. It was proper for Dudley Law Firm to pay David $500 as a referral fee.

II. Dudley Law Firm does estate planning work. One of the lawyers asked Dudley to draft a will for a client. The lawyer does review the work and is ultimately responsible for the work product. The lawyer is subject to discipline for assisting David, a nonlawyer, to engage in the unauthorized practice of law.

III. Dudley Law Firm added David into its retirement plan. The plan is funded in part by legal fees from the firm's lawyers. It is acceptable for the Firm to include David within the retirement plan.

IV. Dudley Law Firm agreed to give David a stock option to pay him for his hard work. The stock options will allow David to buy shares of the Firm's stock at a cheap price. It is fine for David to receive compensation in this manner.

A. I, II, III, and IV.

B. III and IV only.

C. III only.

D. None of the above.

45. Client hired lawyer for a small claims action in state court. Lawyer considered the case to be "small potatoes" so he did not work on it extensively. When Client called to check on the case, Lawyer finally looked at the file. Lawyer realized that he missed a filing deadline which severely prejudiced the client's rights. Lawyer knew that the maximum amount of recovery in small claims court is $10,000. Lawyer was embarrassed by the missed deadline and decided it was best to simply tell Client that they won. Lawyer paid client $10,000 which was the full amount to which Client would have been entitled. Is Lawyer subject to discipline?

   A. No, because Lawyer gave Client $10,000 which was the most Client could have received for the claim. Client was not damaged.

   B. Yes, but only if Client fails to take the $10,000.

   C. No, because Client has an action in legal malpractice against Lawyer in addition to the $10,000 amount for the claim.

   D. Yes, because Lawyer has been dishonest with Client about what actually happened in the case.

46. Client hired Lawyer for a complex child custody case. About mid-way through the case, Client became dissatisfied with Lawyer's strategies on the case and Client fired Lawyer. Client properly paid Lawyer the amount due and owing on the matter up to that point and asked Lawyer to return the file. Client asked Lawyer to provide Client his whole file, including the research, all drafts of papers filed and other documents. Under the ethics rules, what is Lawyer required to turn over to Client?

   A. Only the document drafts, but not the finished product which would include the final legal and fact memoranda.

   B. Only the final product lawyer produced for Client, but not the drafts of documents.

   C. Lawyer does not have to produce Client's file to Client because Client ended the relationship.

D. The full file, including drafts and final work product, regardless of the reason why the Lawyer was discharged.

47. Judge is a trial court judge in State A. Judge is married to a lawyer who is a partner in a law firm. The law firm just awarded the Judge's husband a free ski trip to Utah as a bonus for being the top billing attorney at the firm. Can the Judge allow her husband to accept the trip and take her on the ski vacation?

    A. Yes, but only if Judge reports the vacation as a prize that exceeds $150 in value.

    B. Yes, unless giving partner the bonus trip could be perceived by the public as an attempt to influence a judge.

    C. No, because husband may later appear as an attorney in the court where Judge presides.

    D. Yes, because the prize was won by Judge's husband and not Judge herself.

48. Sam just finished law school and is applying to the state bar of his jurisdiction. Sam had a law school professor who is not licensed in the state in which Sam is applying for his license, but the professor is a licensed attorney in another jurisdiction. Sam asked his professor whether his professor would be willing to fill out Sam's moral character and fitness questionnaire. The questionnaire asked about Sam's fitness to practice law. Specifically, the law professor had to answer several questions about Sam's character for truthfulness. The professor knew that Sam had an ethics issue come up during law school concerning Sam's legal writing course. The professor knew that it resolved in Sam's favor, but the professor was unsure as to whether the professor should disclose the ethics issue. The professor was not on the ethics committee which investigated the issue against Sam. How should the law professor respond to the questionnaire?

    A. The professor should simply disregard that particular question given that the professor was not on the ethics committee at the time of the allegations against Sam.

B. The professor should describe the knowledge the professor has about Sam, including providing a description about what the law professor knows about the ethics issue.

C. The law professor should not disclose Sam's ethics issue unless the law professor obtains Sam's informed consent for the disclosure.

D. The law professor is not under any obligation to fill out the questionnaire as the law professor is not licensed in the jurisdiction in which Sam is applying.

49. Attorney has been in practice for two years. She attended a seminar at Yale Law school. During her two-years as a trial attorney, she won two jury trials and three bench trials. She placed an ad in the local bar magazine under the subject heading, "Litigators Weekly." Her ad stated in relevant part: "Litigation Attorney, Yale-trained; Has Won Every Trial." Which of the following make Attorney subject to discipline?

I. Placing an ad in the section entitled "Litigators Weekly" as Attorney is not a full-fledged "litigator" and this is a misleading statement in a bar magazine.

II. Describing herself as a "Litigation Attorney" in the ad.

III. Stating that she was "Yale-trained."

IV. Making a claim that she had "Won Every Trial."

A. None of the above.

B. I, II, III, and IV.

C. III and IV only.

D. IV only.

50. Client obtained a divorce from Husband two years ago. Husband was ordered to pay child support of $2000 per month. Husband failed to pay the $2000 a month payments for 10 months in a row so Husband owed Client $20,000 in back child support. Client had no money to pay another lawyer. Lawyer agreed to take Client's case under a contingency fee agreement in order to enforce the judgment against the Husband for the child support. At the end of the

case, Lawyer would be entitled to $6000 in fees. Is Lawyer subject to discipline?

A. Yes, because Lawyer is not permitted to charge client a contingency fee in a family law case.

B. No, unless $6,000 violates Rule 1.5 for being an unreasonable fee for this type of matter.

C. Yes, because Lawyer took a percentage of a child support award which negatively impacts Client's children.

D. No, because Client was unable to pay any additional legal fees.

51. Lawyer regularly represented an elderly man, Mr. Smith. Mr. Smith wanted to put $600,000 into an investment that would produce income fairly quickly. Lawyer wanted to contribute his own funds and work with Client to buy an apartment building. Lawyer would put up $100,000 and Mr. Smith would put up $600,000. Lawyer carefully drafted the purchase documents and also drafted a document that explained the business arrangement between Lawyer and Mr. Smith in detail. Lawyer suggested that Mr. Smith have another lawyer review the transaction documents but Mr. Smith did not feel it was necessary. Did Lawyer act correctly?

A. Yes, because a lawyer is allowed to do business with a client.

B. No, because a lawyer is not allowed to do business with a client.

C. Yes, because Lawyer was required to obtain the informed written consent of Mr. Smith prior to proceeding.

D. No, because the lawyer drafted the documents upon which the transaction was based.

52. Attorney has represented Businessman for several years in creating venture capital corporations to obtain investments for Real Estate Investments. The transactions have been very lucrative for both Businessman and Attorney.

Recently, Businessman asked Attorney to represent him in the sale of one of the corporations for the price of $12 million dollars. ABC Company was prepared to purchase the company. During a confidential conversation in Attorney's office, Attorney asked Businessman whether he obtained the appropriate appraisal letters to establish the value of the corporation. Businessman told Attorney he did have such appraisal letters. But then he added: "I had those forged by a friend of mine, just like I did for our prior transactions." What actions should Attorney take now?

I. Report Businessman to the police because Attorney has actual knowledge that Businessman committed fraud.

II. Warn the potential buyer about the fraudulent appraisals.

III. Inform the prior client/s about the fraudulent appraisals.

IV. Refuse to represent Businessman in the present sale.

A. None of the above.

B. II, III, and IV only.

C. IV only.

D. I, II, III, and IV.

53. A few months ago, Attorney represented Client in the sale of Client's business. Client sold the business to Buyer. Buyer showed up at Attorney's office alleging that Client made various untrue statements about the value of the business. Buyer then alleged that Attorney had knowledge of the fraud. Buyer threatened to bring suit against both Attorney and Client. Attorney had information to prove that he was not involved in any fraudulent scheme with Client, but it would involve Attorney disclosing confidential information that Client told him. Can Attorney tell Buyer about the fact without the consent of Client?

A. Yes, Lawyer should disclose the confidential information to protect himself.

B. No, Lawyer would not be entitled to disclose confidential information learned within the attorney-client relationship without Client's consent.

C. Yes, even if the disclosure of information may subject Client to criminal liability for his actions because Lawyer is entitled to protect himself.

D. No, if disclosing such confidential information might harm Client.

54. Defendant is on trial for burglary. Defendant hired Attorney to defend him at the upcoming trial. Defendant states that on the night of the alleged burglary, he was at home with this girlfriend. Attorney interviews Defendant's girlfriend and she also states that Defendant was with her on the night of the alleged burglary. Attorney suspects that both Client and Client's girlfriend are lying, but he does not know for sure. Further, both Defendant and his girlfriend want to testify. Can Attorney call Defendant and his girlfriend as witnesses at trial?

A. No, as to both Defendant and his girlfriend.

B. Yes, as to Defendant but no as to his girlfriend.

C. Yes, as to both Defendant and his girlfriend.

D. Defendant cannot testify but his girlfriend can do so.

55. Lawyer just finished an extensive case and settled the case for $1 million dollars. Lawyer was exhausted by all the work and decided to take a vacation to France. Lawyer was planning to be gone for several weeks but Lawyer told his assistant to "manage" the office while she was gone. Lawyer did not tell his assistant to let Client know about the settlement check when it came. During Week 2 of Lawyer's vacation, the settlement check for $1 million dollars arrived. Lawyer's assistant placed the check in the client trust account but did nothing further. Two weeks later, Lawyer came back well-rested and happy. Lawyer notified client that the settlement check was available. By this time, the settlement check had been sitting in the client trust account for several weeks. Did Lawyer handle the matter correctly?

A. Yes, Lawyer handled the matter correctly because she instructed her assistant to "manage" the office while she was gone and her assistant placed the settlement check in the client trust account.

B. Yes, because the client received the money and there was a delay of only a few weeks.

C. No, because Lawyer had a duty to notify the client promptly that the check had arrived. The fact that the client did not know about the check for three weeks violates the ethical rules.

D. No, because Lawyer's assistant was told to "manage" the office and should have driven the check immediately to client upon receipt of the check.

56. Lawyer landed her first job as a law clerk for the senate committee on Equal and Affordable Housing. Lawyer's main project was to draft proposed legislation for the Domestic Equality Act—a legislative act that provided protection for same-sex couples. The act was eventually passed by the Senate, but not until after Lawyer had left her clerkship. A year later, Lawyer was working at her new law firm in State B. A client wanted to enforce the Domestic Equality Act and wanted Lawyer to take on the case. Given Lawyer's prior clerkship, can Lawyer take on the client's case?

A. No, because Lawyer would have a conflict of interest. because of her prior work related to the legislation.

B. Yes, because although Lawyer worked on a project regarding the proposed legislation, she was not advocating on behalf of a specific client. There would be no conflict of interest for a law clerk to later represent a client involving the same legal statute.

C. Yes, but only if another lawyer at the firm worked on the case, and Lawyer was properly screened off from the matter.

D. No, unless the client gives informed, written consent.

57. An innovative new program called, Legal Services Insurance Co., offers consumers a "legal services insurance policy." Consumers pay an annual insurance premium and

then have the option of choosing attorneys from a pre-approved list. Attorney submitted an application and was selected to be on the panel of attorneys who consumers could select for various legal issues. Will Attorney be subject to discipline for being on the panel of providers through the insurance plan?

A. No, because the consumers under the program are allowed to select any lawyer they want to use.

B. Yes, because lawyers are not allowed to use solicitation to obtain clients.

C. No, unless the insurance company targets its advertising directly to consumers who the insurance company knows are in need of legal services.

D. Yes, because the program is nothing more than a referral program which violates the ethical rules.

58. Lawyer has been in negotiations with ABC Corporation in an employment discrimination lawsuit. ABC Corporation has been represented by competent legal counsel throughout the negotiations. Lawyer represents client and client now wants to sue ABC Corporation because ABC Corporation has not yet produced a suitable settlement offer. Lawyer needs to serve the Summons and Complaint on ABC Corporation at ABC Corporation's corporate headquarters. Lawyer directs his paralegal to contact ABC Corporation and to ask them the address for their corporate headquarters. Paralegal does as instructed and calls ABC Corporation. Is Lawyer subject to discipline?

A. Yes, because Lawyer directed her paralegal to contact ABC Corporation and paralegal did not identify the firm at which paralegal worked.

B. Yes, because Lawyer directed her paralegal to contact ABC Corporation and failed to get opposing counsel's consent prior to contacting a represented client.

C. No, because Lawyer had not formally taken legal action against ABC Corporation.

D. No, because the paralegal was only asking a factual question and not a question pertaining to the substance of the lawsuit between the parties.

59. Lawyer represented Client in a land sale contract of Client's house. Mr. B was buying the house from Client. Lawyer facilitated the negotiations on price and drew up the final contract which both Client and Mr. B signed. A few months later, Mr. B was unhappy with certain aspects of the home and felt that Client failed to properly disclose material defects in the home. Lawyer believes that Client did disclose defects in the home and Lawyer recalls being present during a series of meetings where the defects were discussed. Mr. B plans to sue Client. Client asks Lawyer to defend him in the lawsuit. What is the best course of action for Lawyer?

A. Agree to serve as counsel for Client because Lawyer previously represented Client and it makes the most sense for Lawyer to continue in the representation.

B. Indicate to Client that Lawyer cannot take on the representation of Client in the lawsuit because it is likely that Lawyer will be called as a witness at trial on a material aspect of the case.

C. Agree to represent Client because Lawyer can involve the attorney-client privilege if asked to testify at trial.

D. Decline the representation because it is a conflict of interest for Lawyer to testify adversely to Client.

60. Lawyer agreed to represent Client-Corporation, a new upstart software corporation with a bright future. Because Client-Corporation does not yet have cash flow, Lawyer agreed to an alternative fee arrangement where Lawyer would take 1.5% commission on any sales of the software for a period of three years. Lawyer and Client-Corporation documented the agreement and its terms in a written contract. Lawyer also advised Client-Corporation to have another lawyer review the contract. Client-Corporation declined to do so. Lawyer and Client-Corporation executed the agreement. Which of the following statements is true?

A. Lawyer is subject to discipline because Lawyer acquired a personal interest in the subject matter of the representation.

B. Lawyer's fee agreement is acceptable with Client's full informed, written consent.

C. Lawyer is subject to discipline for entering into an alternative fee arrangement with Client-Corporation without having independent counsel agree that the contract was fair and reasonable.

D. Lawyer's contact with Client Corporation is proper.

Sample MPRE Exam 2 Answer Explanations

1. D is the correct answer because it appropriately states the best way to handle this situation: send Plaintiff $20,000, which represents Plaintiff's settlement amount that is not in dispute; Attorney may also move the undisputed portion of the fees that the attorney earned ($3000) into the office account, and retain the disputed $2000 in the Attorney's Trust Account.

   A is incorrect because Attorney may not keep the full $25,000 in the client trust account; Attorney is required to provide the client the client's award and may only retain actual "earned" fees that are undisputed. In this case, that would be the $2000 disputed amount. Further, Attorney cannot transfer $5000 to the Attorney's office account because $2,000 of that money is in dispute. Rule 1.15.

   B is incorrect because Attorney cannot put the entire $25,000 into the Client Trust Account. However, Attorney may choose to send $20,000 to Client, and transfer the undisputed amount ($3000) to Attorney's Office Account, and then retain the disputed $2000 amount in the Attorney's Trust Account. Because this answer choice contains I., which is incorrect, the entire answer is incorrect.

   C is incorrect because the attorney cannot transfer $5000 to the Attorney's office account because $2000 is in dispute. Under Rule 1.15, Attorney must leave any disputed amount in a Trust Account.

2. C is the correct answer because the attorney may make a statement that is consistent with what the public could learn as a matter of public record. Accordingly, the attorney is not providing any information other than what is already available.

   A is incorrect because whether or not the trial has commenced has no bearing on whether an attorney may make public statements or disclosures concerning a trial. Here, the rule that applies is Rule 3.6, which states that an attorney may not make an extrajudicial statement when he or she is participating in a trial where the attorney knows that the statement will be publicly disseminated and potentially prejudice the trial. Whether the trial has commenced has no bearing on the application of Rule 3.6.

B is incorrect because the fact that that the attorney identified a prospective witness by itself is not enough to cause a violation of Rule 3.6. For example, the witness could have been a part of the public record—so the disclosure may not be problematic.

D is wrong because whether or not the jury learns of the statement is irrelevant; the real question is whether the attorney is making a statement that could potentially prejudice the trial with information beyond that which is publicly known.

3. C is the correct answer. The Prosecutor cannot assert personal opinions about the Witnesses in a case.

   A is wrong because the Prosecutor didn't state the beliefs of the jury, the Prosecutor stated the Prosecutor's OWN beliefs. The Prosecutor is allowed to make arguments about what the jury should and should not do, but may not impose his or her personal views on the matter. Rule 3.8 goes into the special duties of a prosecutor at trial, which go above and beyond attorney's regular duties of candor and honesty. A prosecutor must be fair and cannot seek to influence the jury with his or her own opinions.

   B is wrong because even if the Prosecutor stated the testimony accurately, the Prosecutor gave his or her personal opinion of the testimony.

   D is incorrect because even if the Prosecutor believes that the witness is lying, the Prosecutor cannot state his or her own personal opinion.

4. D is correct. The attorney may delay the trial as long as the Client will not be prejudiced. The time delay is not overly

long and there's nothing in the facts to suggest that the client will be prejudiced by the delay.

A is incorrect because the ethical rules pertaining to an attorney expediting litigation make no distinction between criminal and civil trials. Under Rule 3.2, an attorney has a duty to expedite litigation consistent with the client's interests; an attorney also has a duty of diligence under Rule 1.3. Here, whether the matter is a criminal or civil trial does not impact the application of this rule.

B is incorrect. Although an attorney should manage her calendar so that her cases can be tried promptly, the attorney would not automatically violate Rule 3.2 by moving the trial several months only because of a scheduling conflict. Rule 3.2 talks about the "prejudice" to the client. As long as the delay does not prejudice the client, there is no violation of 3.2.

C is incorrect because the duty to expedite trials exists in both court-appointed and regular trial scenarios. There are not heightened duties because the attorney is court-appointed.

5. D is the correct answer because Bonny could act as Adam's lawyer as long as Jeff is properly screened and not allowed to participate in the case, and Smith & Smith informs Carl of the steps taken to prevent Jeff from participating in the case.

   A is incorrect because it does not apply correctly the Former Client Conflict rule. Under Rule 1.9, a Former Client conflict exists if Jeff, or if any imputation, Jeff's firm, represented Carl in the former suit. The legal question is whether Jeff's former representation of Carl in the suit would be imputed to the law firm where Jeff is now going to work, and where Bonny does work. Under 1.10, Imputation of Conflicts, the Former Client Conflict would be imputed to the firm. Now the question is whether the imputation of the conflict can be waived. Ideally, a firm will request the former client's consent, but it is not technically required by the Model Rules. The firm can screen Jeff from any discussion, files or interaction with the case so that Bonny could represent

Adam in the matter. Pursuant to the screening requirements of 1.10, the firm would need to send Carl notice of the screening, but Carl would not technically need to consent for the representation to proceed. Of course, Adam would also need to consent to the representation after disclosure of the conflict. A is incorrect because the rules (Rules 1.9 and 1.10) contemplate lawyers moving firms, and the rules do not automatically prohibit both lawyers from the representation.

B is wrong because Jeff could not represent Adam in any scenario since he was the opposing attorney in the same matter.

C is wrong because Jeff could not represent Adam, given that he represented Carl. Also, Jeff would be precluded from offering any information to Bonny, and would need to be completely screened from the case under Rule 1.10.

6. C is the correct answer because Lawyer had a duty to supervise a non-lawyer, the paralegal, under Rule 5.1, Duties of a Supervising Attorney. Rule 5.1 requires Lawyer to review any work by a non-lawyer, regardless of the competence of the non-lawyer. Even if the paralegal had filed such responses many times before, Lawyer would still be required to review and sign off on the work.

   A is incorrect because Rule 5.1 requires Lawyer to review any work by a non-lawyer, regardless of the competence of the non-lawyer. Lawyer would still be required to review and sign off on the work as the work was ultimately Lawyer's responsibility.

   B is incorrect because having an important "deadline" does not excuse Lawyer from carrying out the duty to supervise the work of a non-lawyer.

   D is incorrect because it misstates the issue. The issue is the duty of Lawyer to properly supervise a non-lawyer's work; there are not enough facts in the question to determine whether or not Lawyer diligently handled the discovery responses on behalf of client under Rule 1.3, Diligence.

7. A is the correct answer here because the key fact is that disclosure would be detrimental to the client's best interests. Further, the lawyer is under no duty to disclose the perjury, which doesn't involve either his client or the present matter. There would be no breach of the duty of candor to the tribunal. Rule 3.3.

   B is incorrect because although this is one of the reasons why disclosure need not be made, it is not the best reason. The main reason for non-disclosure would be to protect the current client's case.

   C is incorrect, yet it will undoubtedly be an attractive answer. Here, the attorney has knowledge that the opposing party perpetrated fraud. Although the attorney could say something—if the fact of the perjury would not hurt his own client's case—the attorney is not required to say anything to the court. This is not a situation involving dishonesty or lying in this particular action. And, because disclosure would hurt his client, the attorney cannot disclose to the tribunal.

   D is incorrect because a lawyer cannot disclose contrary to his client's best interests.

8. A is the correct answer here. As long as the attorney reasonably believes that a crime was committed, and there is no breach of the attorney's duty of confidentiality to her current client, the attorney can disclose the information. This question is really testing whether you understand that the duty of confidentiality is between the attorney and the current client. Rule 1.6. The facts suggest that the plaintiff/client consented to the disclosure—thereby indicating that there was no breach of the duty of confidentiality. At that moment, the attorney can disclose.

   B is incorrect because the attorney was not required to report knowledge of the criminal conduct of the defendant. The only time an attorney is required to report a crime is when it falls into the exceptions of Rule 1.6, such as death or bodily harm, or a crime to financial interests. Here, it was the Defendant's crime—unrelated to the present case. The attorney had no duty to report.

C is incorrect because the attorney did not have to "know" of a prior crime; the attorney only needed "reasonable belief."

D is incorrect because the duty to report a crime is not contingent on whether a matter is pending or completed. If the correct circumstances exist, an attorney must report a crime even if a matter is pending.

9. C is correct: the attorney will be called as a witness on a contested issue. This answer correctly follows Rule 3.7.

   A is incorrect because if the attorney is likely to be a witness in a matter, the attorney should not take on representation where he or she will be called as a witness. Rule 3.7 states that a lawyer shall not act as an advocate in a case where the lawyer knows that he or she will be called as a witness on a contested issue. Here, it is a contested issue, i.e., the capacity of the decedent. If the attorney is a witness, the attorney cannot also be an advocate in the case.

   B is wrong because the attorney knew he would be a witness on a contested issue. Under Rule 3.7, he cannot take on the new matter.

   D is incorrect because he cannot be both a witness and lawyer regardless of his or her testimony, and particularly if the testimony will be adverse to a client's interest.

10. C is correct. Because the partnership would be providing legal services, the relationship is prohibited under Rule 5.4.

   A is incorrect because regardless of the high quality of services, an attorney's partnership with a non-attorney is prohibited. Under Rule 5.4, a lawyer cannot partner with a non-lawyer if any of their activities involve legal services. Here, there will be legal services provided, so the partnership is prohibited regardless of the quality of the services.

   B is incorrect because the fact that the attorney receives fees for non-legal services does not change the fact that they are both providing legal services in violation of Rule 5.4.

   D is incorrect. Just because the accountant will not provide legal services does not change the fact that Rule 5.4 prohibits the partnership.

11. D is the correct answer here because Bank and Corp have given their informed consent, an approach that actually cures most conflicts under the Model Rules. Here, the facts give even more support that this representation is acceptable; the attorney actually suggested that clients obtain independent counsel.

    A is incorrect because regardless of whether or not an arrangement is customary, there could still be a conflict of interest that would prevent the representation. Here the issue is of a concurrent conflict of interest under Rule 1.7. Where an attorney represents both sides of a transaction, it is considered a conflict of interest. But as with most conflicts, it can be waived if the attorney believes he or she can do the representation effectively and if both clients consent and waive the conflict. Here, the reason for the answer is all wrong.

    B is incorrect because it fails to acknowledge that clients can waive this conflict of interest. Here, the answer choice actually points to a second conflict of interest in this hypothetical, that of a third party payor. Corp will pay the attorney's fees of Bank in this transaction. An attorney is required to remain independent regardless of who is paying the fees. So, this answer choice is incorrect because just because Corp is paying the fees does not mean the attorney cannot represent both parties—as long as both parties waive the conflicts.

    C is incorrect because the fact that they have differing interests—without more—does not prohibit representation with the client's consent.

12. C is correct because Attorney will be subject to discipline because Attorney instructed PI to interview Defendant without disclosing that PI was working for Plaintiff. Defendant was a represented party, and Attorney for Plaintiff would not be allowed to speak with a represented party under the provisions of Rule 4.2. An attorney is required to avoid speaking with a represented party unless the attorney obtains consent from the represented party's attorney. Even if Defendant was not represented, Attorney is required to be clear (and this includes the attorney's

employees or independent contractors) about who the attorney is. An attorney has a duty of candor not only to the court but also to the public.

A is incorrect because following the client's instructions does not negate a rule violation. Watch out for this answer choice—it is usually wrong!

B is incorrect because even if the evidence obtained was good, the way in which attorney went about it violated the ethical rules.

D is incorrect because the attorney can use a PI in any case; the issue here is that the PI would need to disclose who he or she is working for.

13. C is correct because Attorney can either send the Client the full $30,000 or send the client $21,000, and keep the $9,000 in fees (for that portion) in a Trust Account.

    A is incorrect because it states that all options are correct and they are not. This question deals with a client trust account issue and the main thing to remember is that an attorney can put into the attorney's account only actual fees earned that are undisputed. Here, Option I is correct, that attorney can send the client the whole $30,000. The total settlement was for $60,000 so it's not in dispute that at least $30,000 is completely client money. Option II is also correct because Attorney could hold back 10% of the settlement amount as her fee, but the money is in dispute, so Attorney cannot put it anywhere except in a Trust Account. Option III is incorrect because Attorney improperly puts money in her personal account when it is not yet earned because it's in dispute.

    B is incorrect because both Options I and II are allowed.

    D is incorrect because Option III, to transfer any money into a personal account that is in dispute, is wrong.

14. D is correct. Attorney will not be disciplined because the witness had not been subpoenaed by the Defense. If the Defense had subpoenaed the witness and Attorney coerced the witness not to testify, then Attorney would be in violation by improperly influencing a witness, etc.

A is incorrect because Attorney is under no obligation to subpoena a witness knowing that the witness will give unfavorable testimony. Under Rule 3.3, a lawyer has a duty of candor to the tribunal. Here, lawyer does not breach that duty by choosing not to put on a witness. The analysis would be different if the lawyer instructed the witness not to talk to the opposing attorney, or instructed the witness to leave town. But the attorney did not do that here and there is no obligation to call witnesses.

B is incorrect because Attorney did not advise Witt about anything legal in nature, so it does not rise to the level of giving legal advice.

C is incorrect because an attorney is not required to offer inducements to witnesses; in fact, it's the opposite: an attorney cannot induce a witness to testify. An attorney can pay reasonable witness expenses but cannot pay or induce testimony.

15. B is correct. Because the information was gained during a discussion with a potential or prospective client, there are duties that attach between lawyer and prospective client under Rule 1.18.

A is incorrect. When Lennie met with Carrie, a prospective attorney client relationship formed and the attorney-client privilege attached. Lennie would be bound by Rule 1.6, and the only disclosure of that information that would be permitted would be pursuant to the exceptions of Rule 1.6, the Duty of Confidentiality. Here, simply sending copies to the prosecution and defense would violate the 1.6 duty, and thus would be in violation of the rules.

C is incorrect because perpetuating fraud on the court would not be one of the exceptions to Rule 1.6, when Carrie was not Lennie's client.

D is incorrect, as explained above, because it is Carrie's attorney who has an obligation of candor to the court, not Lennie.

16. B is the correct answer because, since Albert was disbarred in California, he cannot practice temporarily in Texas.

Under Rule 5.5, Unauthorized Practice of Law, a lawyer may practice temporarily in another state as long as he or she is not disbarred. Rule 5.5(c). Albert is disbarred so he is not permitted to practice in any other jurisdiction, including Texas.

A is incorrect because the facts state he is only licensed in California.

C is incorrect because working with another attorney—even one who is licensed in the state—does not cure the Rule 5.5 violation.

D is incorrect because he is disbarred; there is no flexibility in the rule. Once disbarred, his privileges to practice end.

17. B is the correct answer because Options I and II are permissible. Option I is permissible because attorneys can take credit cards for payment—nothing in the rules precludes that.

    A is incorrect because Option II, obtaining a bank loan, is not the only correct option. There is nothing to preclude an attorney from obtaining a bank loan for a client.

    C is incorrect because although Options I and II are acceptable, Option III is not. An attorney is prohibited from obtaining publication rights concerning a case under Rule 1.8, i.e., an attorney cannot engage in a business transaction with a client or negotiate rights to literary publication.

    D is incorrect because Options I and II are acceptable; only Option III is not. Option I is permissible because an attorney can accept bank credit cards in payment of attorney's fees. Option II is correct because nothing in the rules precludes an attorney from obtaining a bank loan for the client. Only Option III is incorrect, i.e., an attorney cannot engage in a business transaction with a client or negotiate rights to literary publication.

18. C is correct. The attorney is not counseling the client to avoid arrest; he does not know where the client is and he counseled her to turn herself in.

    A is incorrect because under Rule 1.2, the attorney cannot help perpetuate a client fraud, etc. However, the attorney can provide consultation to the client as to what is the correct action to take.

B is incorrect because an attorney cannot control a client and just because the client refused to accept the attorney's advice does not mean the attorney violated the ethics rules.

D is incorrect because the client does not have to accept the attorney's advice as long as the attorney is not actively perpetuating or contributing to the illegal conduct. Rule 1.2.

19. C is correct; the attorney gave her honest opinion and accurately counseled the clients as to the law.

    A is incorrect because there is no way the attorney could have known or suspected that the parent would use the information to break the law. Unless the attorney has actual knowledge of illegal conduct, the attorney is not required to do anything that would breach the attorney-client relationship/confidence under Rules 1.6 or 1.16.

    B is incorrect because the attorney was not under any obligation to discourage the minor from any activities.

    D is incorrect because the attorney acted appropriately in refusing to provide that information.

20. A is the correct answer because when a case is before a tribunal, court approval is needed for withdrawal, even if the attorney and client both agree they do not want to work together. Rule 1.16.

    B is incorrect because, under Rule 1.16, even if the client agrees, it is still up to the court when a case is before a tribunal.

    C is not correct because whether or not an attorney can permissively withdraw is dependent upon the court's approval when the case is before the tribunal.

    D is incorrect because although prejudice is a ground on which the court could deny the withdrawal request, there are no facts here which support this statement.

21. C is correct; the attorney can rely upon the exception to Rule 1.6 that allows the attorney to reveal confidential information if the attorney is being investigated. A is

incorrect because although the lawyer can in fact use the letter in his defense, this is not the correct reason; the attorney would be using the letter as an exception to the Rule 1.6, Attorney Client Confidentiality rule, i.e., to protect an attorney's rights in a disciplinary proceeding. Attorney would not be able to use the letter for establishing that the client lied.

A is incorrect because the client committing a fraud on the court is actually not an exception to the attorney-client privilege, so revealing the confidential information would not be permitted for this reason.

B is incorrect because although the attorney did learn the facts in confidence, there is an exception to Rule 1.6 that would apply here.

D is incorrect because the attorney would not be prosecuted for perjury for this disclosure; the lawyer did not lie, the client did.

22. B is correct; the attorney cannot respond to the request because the client specifically said not to tell or disclose the information and this information would be client confidences under Rule 1.6.

    A is incorrect because the attorney actually cannot give out the information; the attorney is bound by the client's instructions here and the settlement amounts are not work product.

    C is not correct because the duty of confidentiality extends far beyond the end of the client representation—sometimes even beyond the death of the client, depending on the state.

    D is incorrect because the fact that the attorney believes the disclosure would benefit the client is not a reason that would allow the attorney to disclose under Rule 1.6.

23. B is correct because an attorney may not, pursuant to Rule 3.4, counsel someone to destroy potentially relevant evidence. If the records are potentially relevant in future litigation, the attorney is duty-bound to instruct the client not to destroy the records.

A is incorrect because whether litigation is pending or not is irrelevant to whether the attorney should tell the client not to destroy evidence. Rule 3.4.

C is incorrect because it does not have to be certain that the company was the manufacturer—just potentially relevant.

D is incorrect because, even if the company has established a shredding policy, the instant the records become potentially relevant, the client must not destroy them. Rule 3.4.

24. C is the correct answer because Rule 1.8(h)(1) requires that you advise the client in writing that they can seek independent legal representation before deciding to enter into the settlement agreement.

    A is not correct because an attorney under Rule 1.8(h)(1) is not permitted to prospectively have the client waive malpractice liability without the client having an independent attorney review the agreement.

    B is incorrect because Billy does not have to be represented in negotiating the settlement agreement. Instead, the rule requires that the client be advised in writing that Billy should seek independent legal representation.

    D is incorrect because regardless of whether the attorney believes the agreement is fair, the attorney must provide written advice to have an independent lawyer review.

25. C is correct because it correctly states that the attorney can state what is in their pleadings, and the attorney can state what witnesses may be helpful pursuant to Rule 3.6.

    A is incorrect because the fact that Cara was no longer in love with Daniel at the time Laura was conceived is completely irrelevant. This is an incorrect premise.

    B is incorrect because although it is proper to inquire about possible witnesses, this reason is not the only correct answer. Rule 3.6 states that you can inquire as to facts that are a matter of public record, and about information/witnesses that may have needed information.

D is incorrect because a lawyer can inquire about facts that are a matter of public record.

26. A is correct. Although students may initially assume that this would violate the conflicts of interest provision of Rule 1.7, the truth is that most conflicts can be waived with informed consent and waiver. If both clients give informed consent, the attorney may be able to represent both clients.

    B is incorrect because it is a conflict of interest issue and not a confidentiality issue.

    C is incorrect because although adverse interests go to the fact that there is a conflict of interest, the conflict can be waived under Rule 1.7.

    D is incorrect because even adverse interests can be waived (although it is not likely to happen).

27. C is correct because Penny's testimony was true, so there was no putting forth of false testimony in violation of the ethics rules here.

    A is not correct because an attorney does have a duty to the tribunal to be honest and not present false testimony. But Penny's answer was actually truthful based on the question's phrasing, so A is wrong.

    B is incorrect because an attorney does owe a duty of candor to the tribunal under Rule 3.3, but the testimony was technically truthful.

    D is incorrect because here, there was no false testimony. So although an attorney would need to remedy false testimony, here, there was none.

28. A is the correct answer because under Rule 1.7, this is a concurrent conflict of interest where the interests of the parties are adverse to each other. Here, objectively, the attorney cannot state that the attorney believes he can represent both brothers. Such joint representations are always fraught with danger; the facts here suggest that their interests are already not aligned, so the attorney cannot represent the brothers here.

B is incorrect because the ethical rules do not always prohibit joint representations. They can occur with client consent, as long as it is objectively reasonable that the attorney could represent both.

C is incorrect because the rule considers "interests" in a broad sense; the testimony does not have to be directly conflicting. Here, the likelihood that Benji will get leniency is enough to constitute divergent interests.

D is incorrect because client consent and waiver will not cure a conflict of interest when there is direct adversity.

29. D is correct because the waiver must be requested prior to the attorney beginning the representation with Harry.

A is incorrect because Adam has not acted properly. Here, Wilma is a former client, and pursuant to Rule 1.9, an attorney cannot take on a new client without consent when it would be materially adverse to a former client in a substantially related case. Here, Adam would have violated Rule 1.9 because the interests were adverse and he learned confidential information during his initial representation that would have hurt his former client if he continued to represent Harry. Further, even if he wanted to obtain consent, he needed to ask for this before his representation of Harry began. Here, he asked after and that violates Rule 1.7.

B is incorrect because although a waiver can sometimes cure a conflict of interest, the present conflict cannot be cured because the attorney learned confidential information in the prior representation that will hurt Wilma. Under 1.9, he cannot take the case.

C is incorrect because a waiver does not have to be notarized to be valid.

30. C is correct because Option II, that she can consider her financial hardship as a ground for not taking an appointment, is correct.

A is incorrect because not all the options are correct. Under Rule 6.2, Accepting Judicial Appointments, an attorney may not decline an appointment simply because her practice areas are elsewhere. Option II is correct because financial hardship is a ground for not taking a case. II and IV are incorrect because injuring a reputation is not a ground for not taking an appointment, nor is offending clients a ground.

B is incorrect because Option II is correct.

D is not correct because only Option II is correct.

31. B is correct because Rule 8.1 states that you cannot make a false statement on a bar application or on a recommendation for someone on a bar application. Linda would be making a false statement if she said her cousin is honest.

    A is incorrect because Linda cannot write the letter, but not because she's not a member of State B. She doesn't have to be a member of State B in order to write a letter of bar admission—she just needs to be a member of a state bar. She would not be allowed to write a letter in this situation because she believes her cousin is dishonest and she could not truthfully state otherwise.

    C is not correct because her opinion is exactly what the Bar Examiners want; she has to state it honestly under Rule 8.1.

    D is incorrect because State B (and any State Bar) relies upon recommendations about a lawyer's good moral character, and not on their own opinion.

32. A is the correct answer here because although an attorney must typically keep all client confidences, the duty of confidentiality does have some exceptions under Rule 1.6. Pursuant to Rule 1.6, one exception is if the client is going to engage in activities that would be the commission of a future crime and/or result in the client's substantial bodily harm. Suicide would fall into both categories and would be a reason why the attorney could disclose the information to authorities.

    B is incorrect because this scenario involves the attorney-client privilege regarding an attorney's ethical rules, not the evidentiary privilege used at trial.

    C is incorrect because the attorney does not have to know that the client attempted suicide in the past.

D is incorrect because regardless of whether disclosure would help client's case, the attorney cannot disclose unless the exceptions of Rule 1.6 are met.

33. A is the correct answer here because an attorney for a corporation is allowed to withdraw in certain circumstances under Rule 1.16, and one of them is when a lawyer reasonably believes that actions must be criminal. A correctly states the standard.

    B is incorrect because it misstates Rule 1.16; mandatory withdrawal is not required. Withdrawal is permitted as stated in A.

    C is incorrect because the lawyer can withdraw under Rule 1.16. The lawyer is not breaching or disclosing any confidential information.

    D is incorrect because Corp's ability to complete the filing in a timely fashion is not a ground for consideration when determining withdrawal options.

34. C is the correct answer because it properly captures what the rule requires, i.e., that the statement was false. Rules 4.1; 3.3.

    A is not correct because Beta did not know the statement was false, and the rules requiring honesty of the attorney to the tribunal and others, i.e., Rule 4.1 and Rule 3.3, state that the attorney must knowingly make a false statement of fact. The facts indicate that Beta did not know this to be a misstatement of fact.

    B is incorrect, but it is a difficult one to decipher. The answer states that Beta did not know the statement was "true," but that's not the language of the rule/s. Rules 4.1 and 3.3 state that the lawyer must know the statement is false.

    D is incorrect because the fact that Beta reiterated the brief does not get at the heart of the issue, i.e., whether he spoke dishonestly and whether he knew that the fact was false.

35. C is correct because permissive withdrawal is just that: permissive. It is often up to the judge to determine whether withdrawal is even allowed. The fact that the client did not

pay his or fees is not enough to establish or justify withdrawal in every case.

A is incorrect because it misstates the standard in the rules regarding withdrawal. Although a financial burden would be one possible reason for permissive withdrawal, there is no balancing test in the rule about having to assess whether the financial burden of "continuing the representation would be substantially greater than the parties anticipated . . ." This is not a correct statement of a ground for permissive withdrawal under Rule 1.16.

B is not correct because client consent at the beginning of representation would not be appropriate to rely on under Rule 1.16.

D is incorrect because it improperly states the standard of Rule 1.16.

36. D is the correct answer because the representation would not be allowed unless Attorney informed Defendant and Defendant consented to the payment by his Aunt.

A is incorrect. The fact that the third party payor's (the Aunt's) goals are similar to Defendant's goals does not address the issue here: whether the lawyer has a conflict of interest due to having a third party pay the client's fees. Rule 1.8. Having a third party payor is a conflict under Rule 1.8. The conflict can be waived by telling the client and having the client agree to the payment, and also by ensuring that the lawyer's judgment will not be influenced by a third party paying the bill/s.

B is incorrect because reducing the charges does not waive or eliminate the conflict of interest.

C is incorrect because it is possible for Aunt to pay the bills, but the client needs to be aware of and consent to such third party payment under Rule 1.8.

37. A is the correct answer because even though there is a conflict of interest under Rule 1.7, the conflict can be waived by client consent and written waiver. Here, not only was there consent and waiver but the clients also consulted with

independent counsel—which goes to the issue of a knowing and intelligent waiver.

B is incorrect because whether an arrangement is customary in the community has no bearing on whether the ethical rules have been violated.

C is incorrect because the fact that Corp is paying the fees does nothing to impact the dual representation conflict under Rule 1.7. A waiver is required.

D is incorrect because the fact that they have different interests actually makes it more problematic that there is a dual representation, not less. The concurrent conflict would still exist under Rule 1.7 precisely because they have opposing interests in the same transaction.

38. D is the correct answer because Attorney would be disciplined for violating Rule 1.6. There are no exceptions that fit this situation and Attorney would not be permitted to disclose the confidential information of his client.

A is incorrect because the attorney-client privilege can last (depending on the state) beyond the death of the client, so the client's death is not enough to suggest that the lawyer can disclose the confidential information under Rule 1.6.

B is incorrect because the legal issue is whether Attorney has grounds to breach his duty of confidentiality to his client. There is a test that involves balancing the relative interests between Joe and the Robber.

C is incorrect because the crime-fraud exception does not apply; there is not a future crime that would be committed by the disclosure.

39. C is correct. Dana will not be liable for malpractice because the client did not suffer harm in terms of the result, but she will be disciplined for violating Rule 1.1 because she did act without competence in failing to research the law.

A is incorrect because although Dana will be sanctioned for incompetence under Rule 1.1, she will not be liable for malpractice because her client was not actually harmed, i.e., he was acquitted, so there was no real damage, which is necessary to prove legal malpractice.

B is incorrect because she did not commit malpractice and she will be sanctioned for incompetence, despite the favorable result.

D is incorrect because she will be sanctioned for incompetence.

40. C is correct because an attorney is allowed to argue against a law or a judicial decision if an attorney has a good faith basis for such an argument, i.e., a good faith argument for reversal of the applicable law. Rule 3.3.

    A is incorrect because although a lawyer typically would not want to argue against current state law on an issue, Rule 3.3 allows the attorney to utilize a case as long as there is a good faith argument that the decision should be reversed.

    B is incorrect because she is not incompetent under Rule 1.1; she knows the decision in the state regarding the legal issue. She wants to argue against it, which is different than saying she doesn't know or understand it.

    D is incorrect because advocating for a client zealously does not mitigate a lawyer's duty to be truthful and open to the court under Rule 3.3.

41. D is correct because she would be permitted to report an attorney even if the attorney was licensed in a jurisdiction different than her own, under Rules 8.3 and 8.4.

    A is incorrect because a judge can report misconduct similarly to an attorney.

    B is incorrect because an attorney and/or judge is allowed to report an ethical violation regardless of what jurisdiction in which the action occurs.

    C is incorrect because she does not have personal knowledge that that there was an ethical violation.

42. C is correct. The attorney has violated the ethics rules because the attorney has not complied with the requirements of Rule 1.16, Withdrawal. Further, the attorney failed to follow the judge's order which "trumps" even Rule 1.16.

A is incorrect because Lacy will be disciplined because she improperly withdrew from the case in violation of the Permissive Withdrawal provisions of Rule 1.16. The professional responsibility rules apply equally to both paying and non-paying clients.

B is incorrect because a lawyer must assess their competence to handle a case *prior* to agreeing to represent the client. Here, Lacy made the determination too late; she should have never taken the case in the first place. Once she agreed to represent the client, she had a duty to carry out that representation to conclusion.

D is incorrect because Rule 1.1 does allow lawyers to "become competent" by either studying or associating with another lawyer. Here, the attorney could gain competence by studying or associating with another attorney.

43. D is correct because under Rule 3.5, an attorney is not allowed to speak to a juror on a pending case.

A is incorrect because it improperly characterizes the issue. The issue is not related to the attorney's competence but whether or not the attorney was permitted to speak with a juror who was on a pending case. Even if the attorney properly explained the legal definition of "intent" he was prohibited from speaking to a juror under Rule 3.5.

B is incorrect because under Rule 3.5, the attorney was not permitted to speak to a juror regardless of the accuracy of his explanation.

C is incorrect because the attorney was not permitted to discuss anything with a juror on a pending case under Rule 3.5.

44. C is correct because the Firm can include David in its retirement plan.

A is incorrect because under I., a Firm cannot pay a referral fee under the Model Rules. Further, II. is incorrect because even though the attorney is a non-lawyer, it appears the attorney is properly supervising the non-lawyer, David. As such, this is acceptable under the Model Rules. III is correct because the firm can include David in the retirement plan.

But IV is not correct because non-lawyers cannot receive stock options in the Firm.

B is incorrect because answer choice III is correct; and answer choice IV is not correct.

D is incorrect because answer choice III is correct.

45. D is the correct answer because Lawyer has been dishonest with Client in violation of Rule 4.1 and failed under Rule 1.4 to properly communicate the situation to Client.

A is incorrect because although Lawyer has "made the client whole" by giving the $10,000 to the Client, Lawyer still failed in his duties of honesty and communication to the Client under Rules 4.1 and 1.4.

B is incorrect because whether Client takes the $10,000 is completely separate from the fact of whether Lawyer violated the ethical rules.

C is incorrect because if Client suffers no actual damages, i.e., Lawyer pays Client the $10,000, then Client could not sustain a malpractice claim because one of the essential elements is that a client suffers damages.

46. D is correct because once an attorney-client relationship ends, Rule 1.16 requires the attorney to give to the client the full file, which can include drafts as well as the final product.

A is incorrect because the fact that the client ends the relationship or the attorney terminates the relationship does not matter under Rule 1.16. The client is always entitled to his or her entire file.

B is incorrect because the client is allowed to receive the entire file, including drafts and final documents.

C is incorrect because a client is always allowed to have the entire client file under Rule 1.16, regardless of whether the client or the attorney ended the relationship.

47. B is the correct answer because it properly states the standard for proper judicial conduct which is that a judge cannot accept anything which might create the appearance of influence or bias.

A is incorrect because the rules of Judicial Conduct always require a judge to make a report of compensation—so the trip here would not be any different than accepting any gift or prize.

C is incorrect. Simply because husband may appear as an attorney at the state court sometime in the future is not enough to disqualify the husband from taking the trip. The judge would always have the option of recusing herself if she was selected to hear a matter on husband's case.

D is incorrect because Judge would be receiving something of benefit even if her husband was awarded the prize.

48. B is correct because law professor is required to answer truthfully in responding to the bar questionnaire as is required by Rule 8.1. The law professor should describe what she knows about Sam's ethics issue.

A is incorrect because the law professor, as a licensed attorney, is required to answer truthfully regardless of the jurisdiction in which she is licensed.

C is incorrect because the law professor has an ethical obligation to answer truthfully under Rule 8.1.

D is incorrect because regardless of where law professor is licensed, law professor is required to comply with 8.1 and answer truthfully.

49. C is correct because only IV. is misleading. Attorney can state she is a "Litigation Attorney" because she is one, and because she is not claiming she is an "expert" (which would be improper). Further, Attorney does appear to have obtained a certification from a Yale seminar so this is objectively verifiable and accurate. However, IV is misleading because Attorney cannot say that she has "won" every trial—because she has lost a bench trial. This statement could be misleading to a consumer in violation of Rule 7.1.

A is incorrect because only IV. is misleading and as such, improper under the ethics rules.

B is incorrect because IV. is misleading and Attorney would be disciplined for stating IV. in the ad.

D is incorrect because not all the options would lead to discipline.

50. B is correct because Lawyer complied with the ethics rules and would not be disciplined as long as the fees were not unreasonably high. Here, the amount of $6000 does not seem unreasonable under Rule 1.5.

A is incorrect because although a lawyer cannot charge a contingent fee in a domestic relations or family law case, a lawyer *can* do so if a lawyer is enforcing a judgment (that has already been negotiated/resolved in court). Here, Lawyer's actions comply with Rule 1.5 because Lawyer is enforcing a prior judgment.

C is incorrect because Lawyer is enforcing a judgment.

D is incorrect because whether the client was able to pay has no bearing on whether the lawyer violated the ethics rules.

51. C is correct because the attorney needed to obtain the client's informed, written consent under Rule 1.8.

A is incorrect because an attorney can enter into a business transaction with a client as long as the attorney meets the requirements of Rule 1.8.

B is incorrect because an attorney can enter into a business transaction with a client as long as the attorney meets the requirements of rule 1.8.

D is incorrect because the lawyer can draft the documents. The key to a Rule 1.8 transaction between lawyer and client is that lawyer explain the transaction, that the transaction is fair and reasonable, that lawyer advise client to seek outside counsel, and that client provide informed, written consent.

52. C is the correct answer because the only proper ethical action is to withdraw from the representation to prevent any future harm. Attorney must withdraw under Rule 1.16 if the client is pursuing fraudulent conduct.

A is incorrect because choice IV is correct. Here, it's important to note that the fact statement says that the

Attorney spoke to the Businessman "in confidence" which means that Rule 1.6, the Duty of Confidentiality, applies.

B is incorrect because II and III are incorrect. Attorney is not allowed to notify the potential purchaser because it would violate the Attorney's duty under Rule 1.6. III is wrong because the client disclosed the information in "confidence" and there is no likely future or current harm so any exceptions to Rule 1.6 do not apply. In addition, IV is also correct as indicated above.

D is an incorrect answer choice given that answer choice IV is correct.

53. C is the correct answer because even though Attorney has a duty of confidentiality to Client, an exception under Rule 1.6 likely applies here. Attorney is preventing a future harm and also defending himself against accusations that Attorney was involved in fraud.

    A is incorrect because whether or not Attorney can disclose the confidential information is dependent on whether an exception to Rule 1.6 applies on the facts of this case. Any exception is not dependent on whether Buyer files suit against Client.

    B is incorrect because even though Attorney owes Client a duty of confidentiality, an exception to Rule 1.6 may apply here.

    D is incorrect because Rule 1.6 contains an exception that may apply even if some harm may come to Client. Although Attorney must take the duty of confidentiality very seriously, the duty does contain exceptions.

54. C is correct because Attorney can have both witnesses testify.

    A is incorrect because Attorney can call both witnesses. Although Attorney suspects that the witnesses may lie, he does not *know* for sure that the witnesses will lie. The standard which would prevent Attorney from calling the witnesses because this would be Attorney putting on false testimony in front of the tribunal. But here, the attorney doesn't know there will be false testimony, so Attorney may present the witnesses.

B is incorrect because Attorney can put both witnesses on the stand at trial.

D is incorrect because Attorney can put both witnesses on the stand.

55. C is the correct answer because under Rule 1.4, Attorney has a duty to communicate with the client, which includes the obligation to notify the client immediately when settlement funds arrive.

    A is incorrect because although Attorney's assistant properly placed the funds in a client trust account, Attorney had an independent duty to promptly notify client of the arrival of the funds under Rule 1.4.

    B is incorrect because whether the client is harmed is irrelevant to a whether Attorney violated the ethics rules.

    D is incorrect because there is no duty to "drive" the funds to the client but there is a duty to "notify" the client promptly upon receipt of the funds.

56. B is correct because Lawyer can work on the case.

    A is incorrect because Lawyer is permitted to work on the matter. As a prior senatorial law clerk, the legal issue is whether Lawyer would have a conflict of interest. Here, however, there is no conflict. Lawyer who worked on the legislation just worked generally on the statute, not for a specific client. Therefore, Lawyer may work on the case.

    C is incorrect because there is no actual conflict of interest.

    D is incorrect because Attorney may work on the case.

57. C is correct because the lawyer can be a part of the program. This is one type of referral program allowed by the rules of professional responsibility as the lawyer has no direct contact with the clients. Pursuant to Rule 7.3 (b), a lawyer is permitted to be a part of a prepaid program.

    A is incorrect because the legal issue is whether a lawyer can be a part of a pre-paid referral program for legal services. This is one exception to the general rule re: lawyer solicitation, etc.

B is incorrect because Rule7.3 states that a lawyer can be a part of a prepaid legal services program. Under such a program, clients can be solicited in person as long as the solicitation for services comes from the program and not the lawyer personally. Because the potential clients sign up for the program, the rules consider this situation differently than an in-person solicitation by a lawyer.

D is incorrect because the legal issue is whether a lawyer can be a part of a pre-paid referral program for legal services. This is one exception to the general rule re: lawyer solicitation, etc. as a prepaid program is permissible.

58. B is the correct answer because under Rule 4.2, a lawyer (or someone who the lawyer directs) who communicates to a party known to be represented by counsel must obtain the opposing lawyer's consent prior to contacting the represented party. Identifying who you are prior to talking with a represented party is always a good idea, but the rule requires that you obtain the consent of the represented party's lawyer.

    A is incorrect because the paralegal (as the agent of the attorney) was required to obtain opposing counsel's consent pursuant to Rule 4.2, Communicating with People Represented by Counsel.

    C is incorrect as the ethics rule applies regardless of the topic about which you discuss. The issue is whether you obtained the opposing attorney's consent.

    D is incorrect because the lawyer (or paralegal) can communicate with the party as long as the lawyer has opposing counsel's consent.

59. B is the correct answer because under Rule 3.7, a lawyer cannot take on a representation if the lawyer believes she will be called as a witness at trial.

    A is incorrect because Lawyer cannot take on the representation because Lawyer will likely be called as a witness, and Rule 3.7 prohibits a lawyer from acting as a witness at trial.

C is incorrect because Lawyer cannot be a trial lawyer in the case and the attorney-client privilege would not apply in this instance given that the negotiations occurred in the presence of a third party, Mr. B.

D is incorrect because the real issue is under Rule 3.7 and this is not a conflict of interest.

60. D is correct because the fee agreement is possible, even though the lawyer has a personal interest in the litigation, because the lawyer complied with the requirements of Rule 1.5 concerning fees. Also Lawyer complied with Rule 1.8 concerning taking a personal interest in the subject matter of the transaction. Rule 1.8 requires that the terms be fair and that the lawyer advises the client to seek independent counsel to review the terms.

A is incorrect because the lawyer will not face discipline here. Although a lawyer generally cannot take a "personal interest" in the subject matter of the litigation, it is permissible as long as the terms are fair and the lawyer suggests that the client obtain independent counsel under Rule 1.8.

B is incorrect because the issue is not about the fee agreement as much as it is about a Rule 1.8 personal conflict of interest regarding the lawyer taking an interest in the outcome of the litigation.

C is incorrect because Lawyer is not subject to discipline.

The End